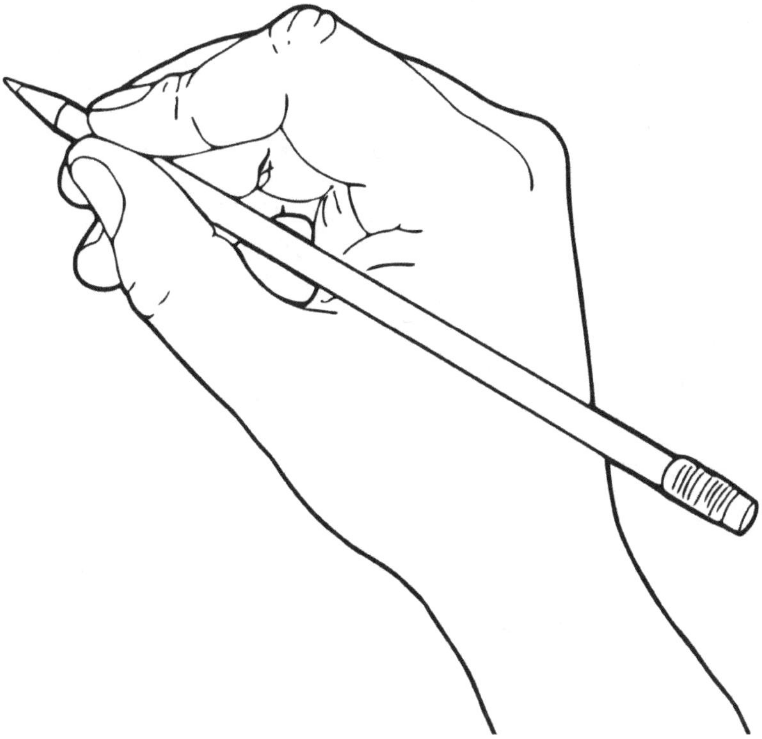

This Notebook belongs to:

____

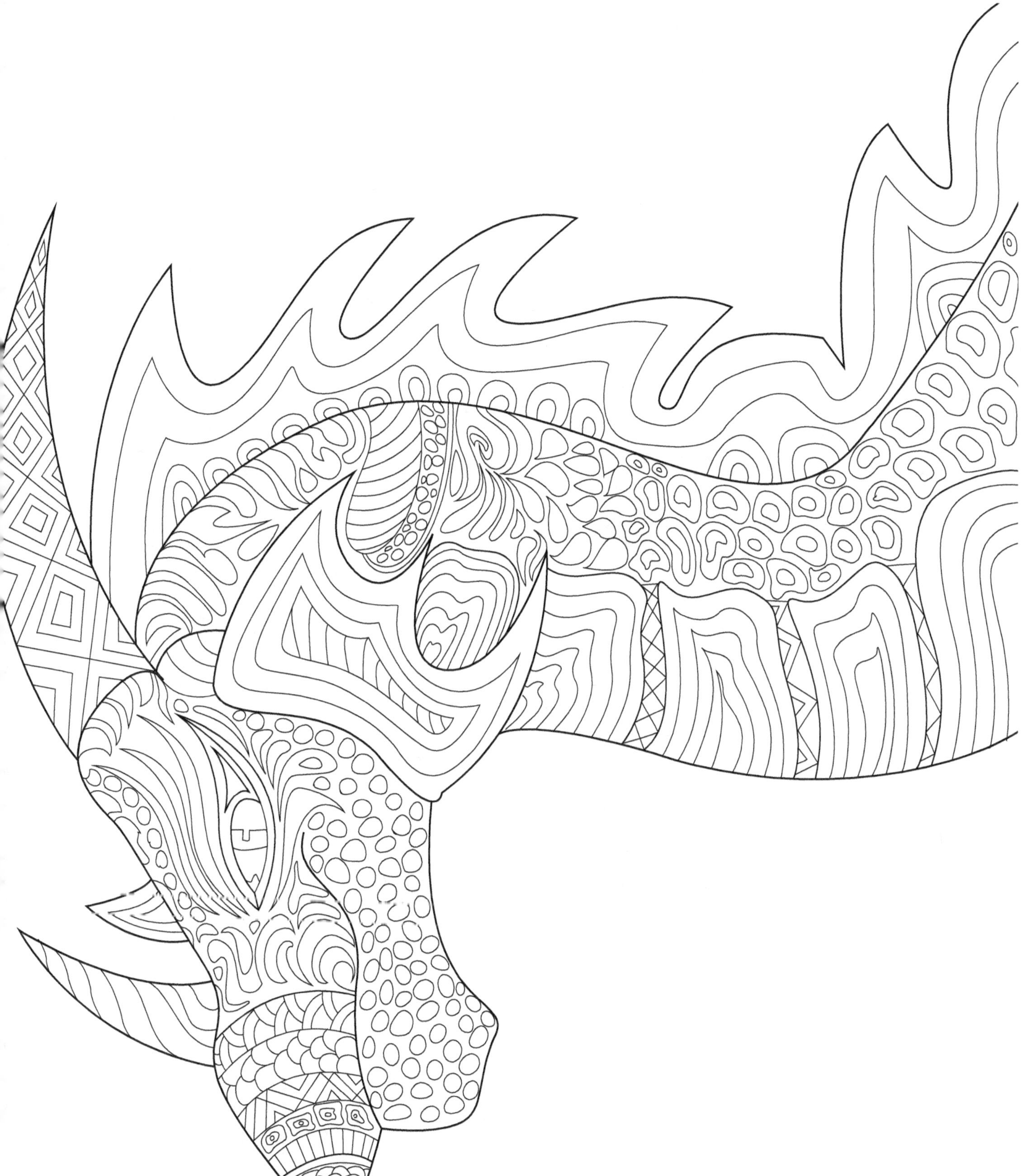

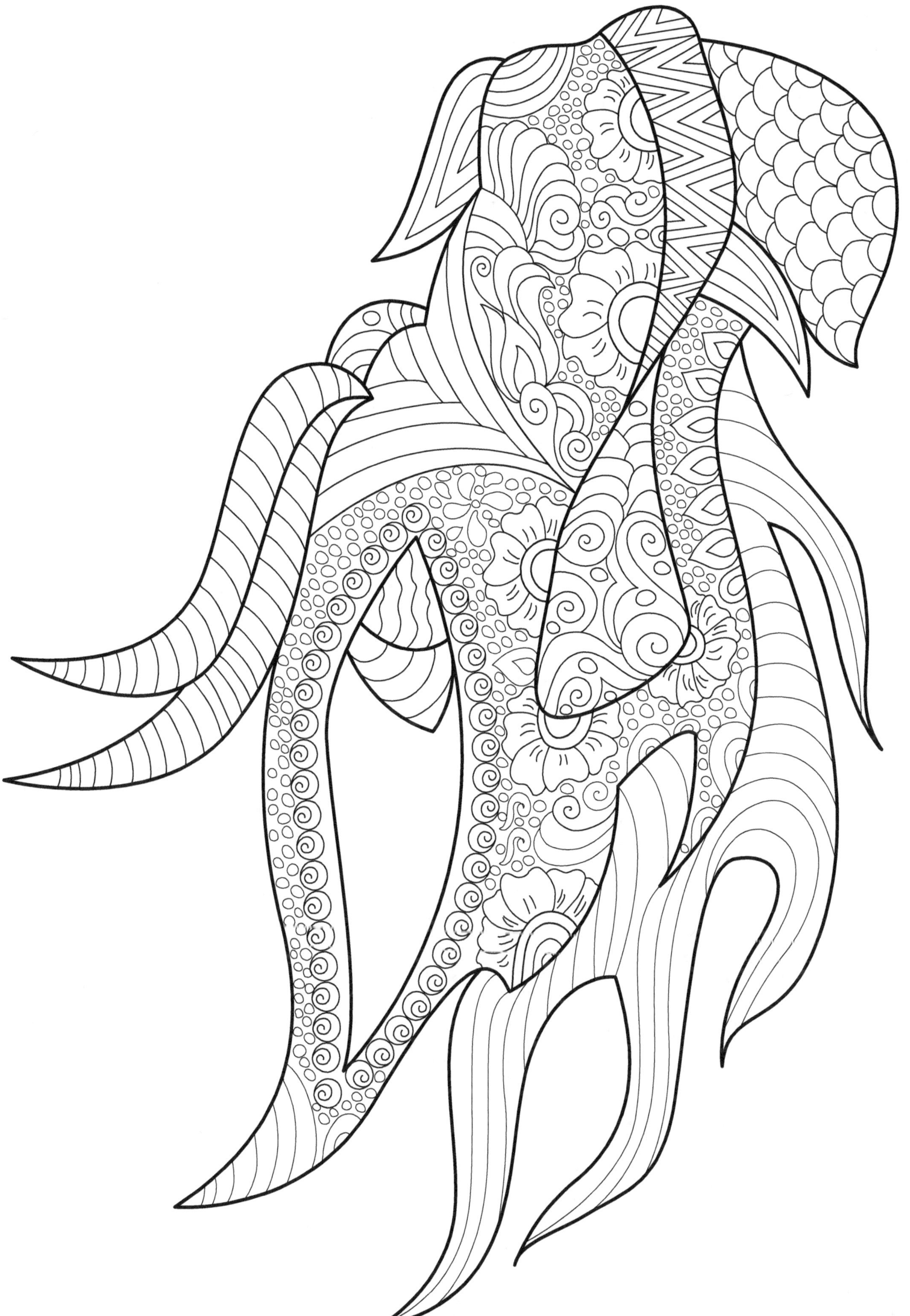

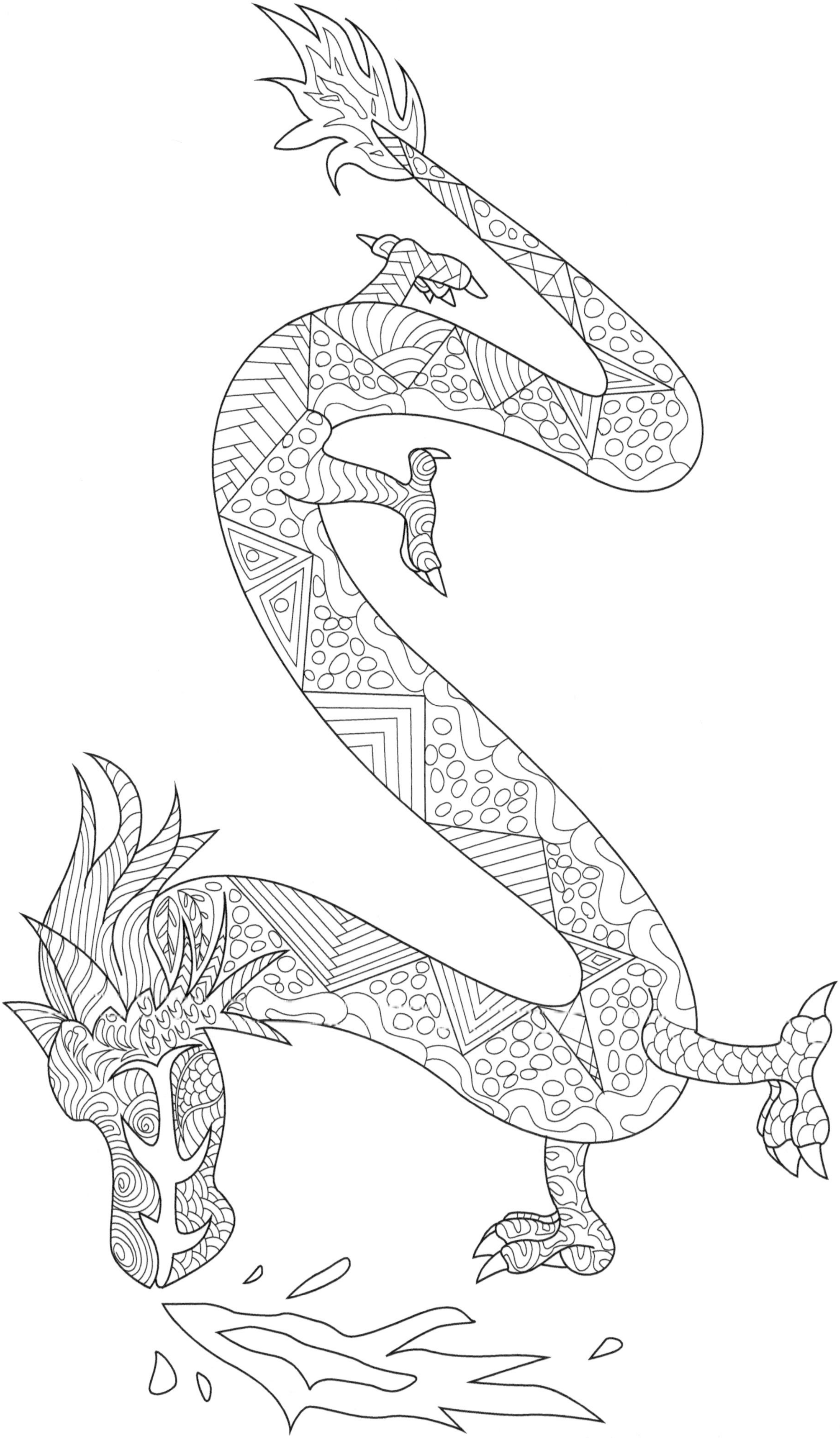

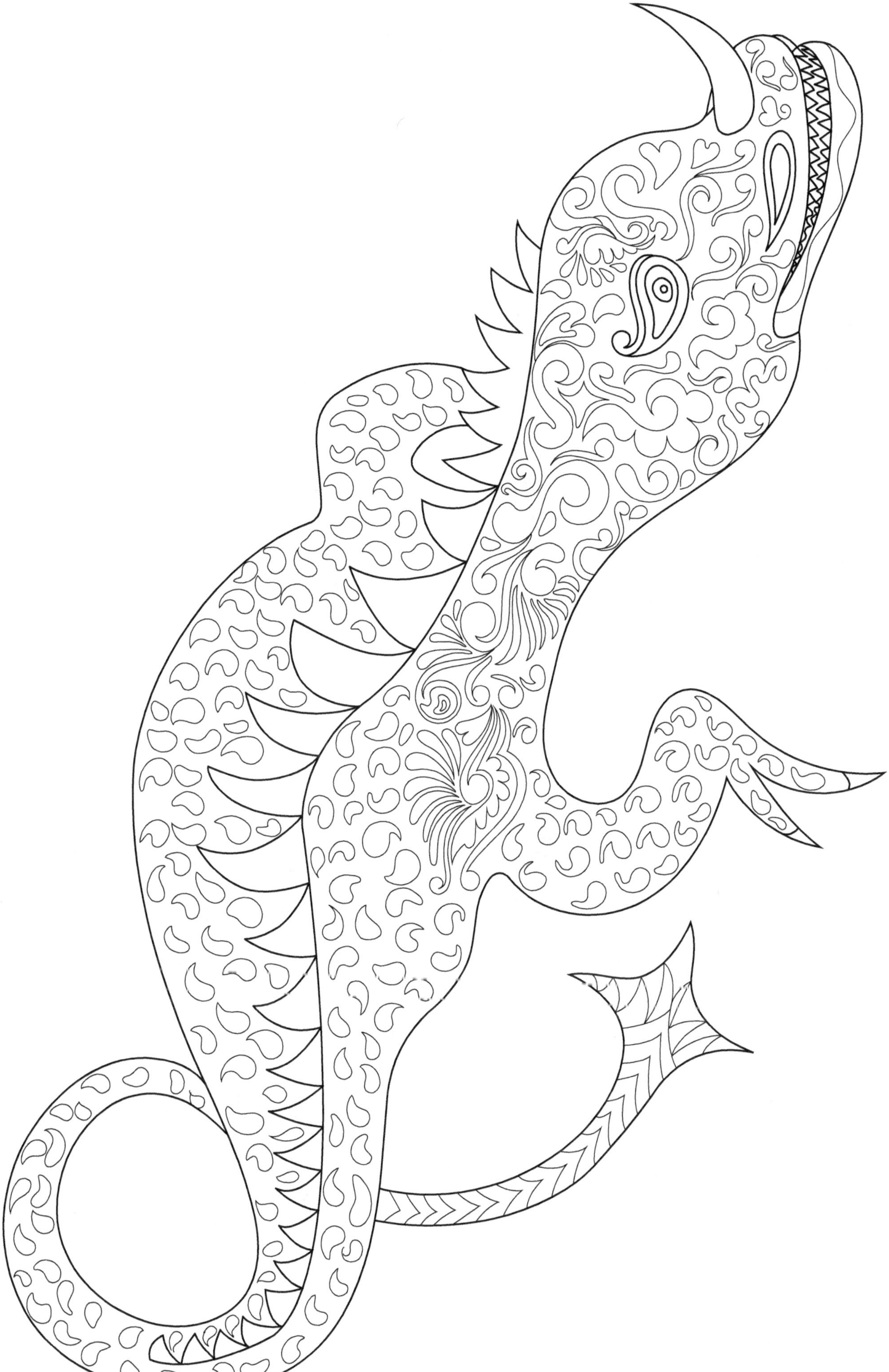

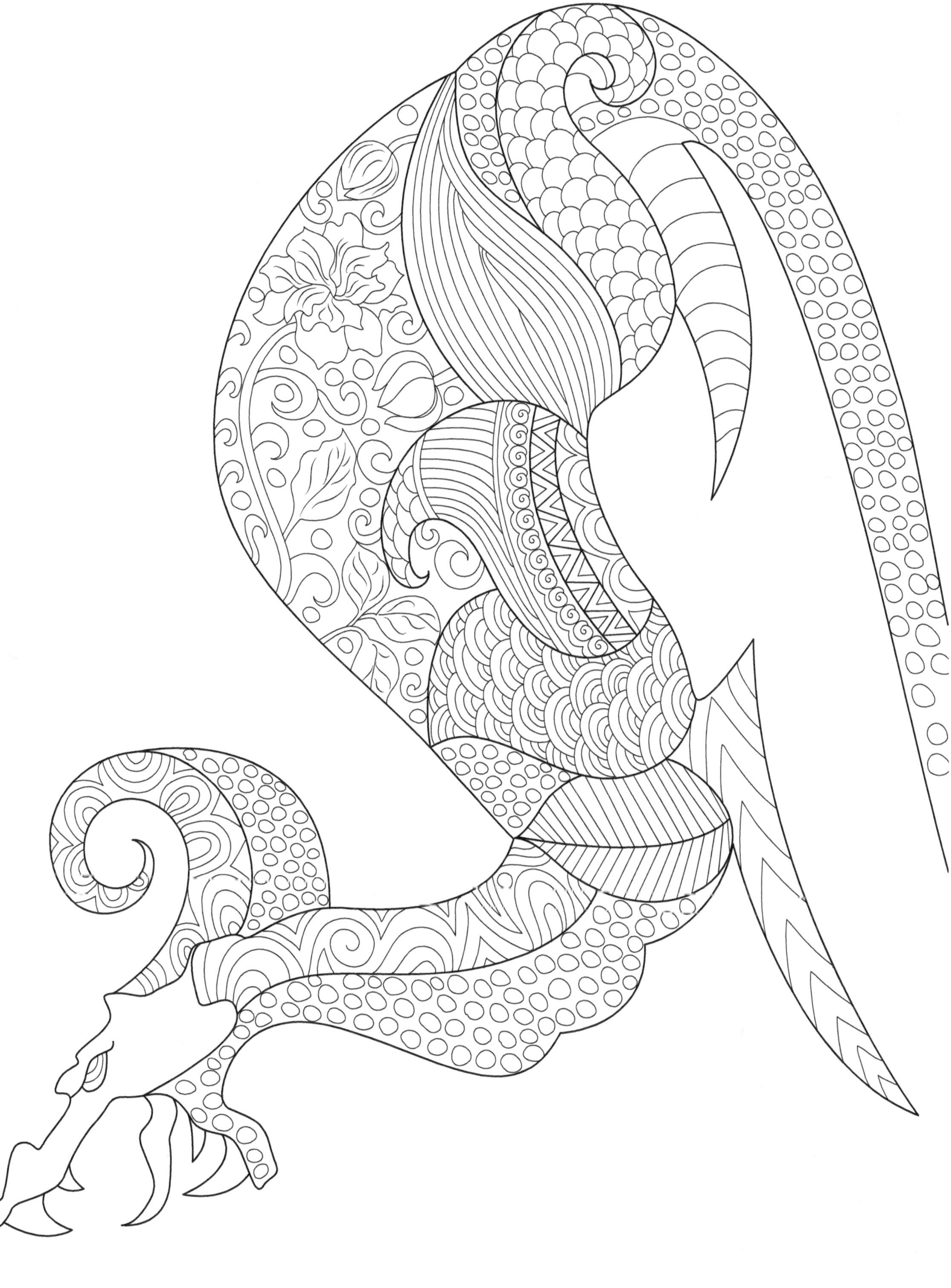

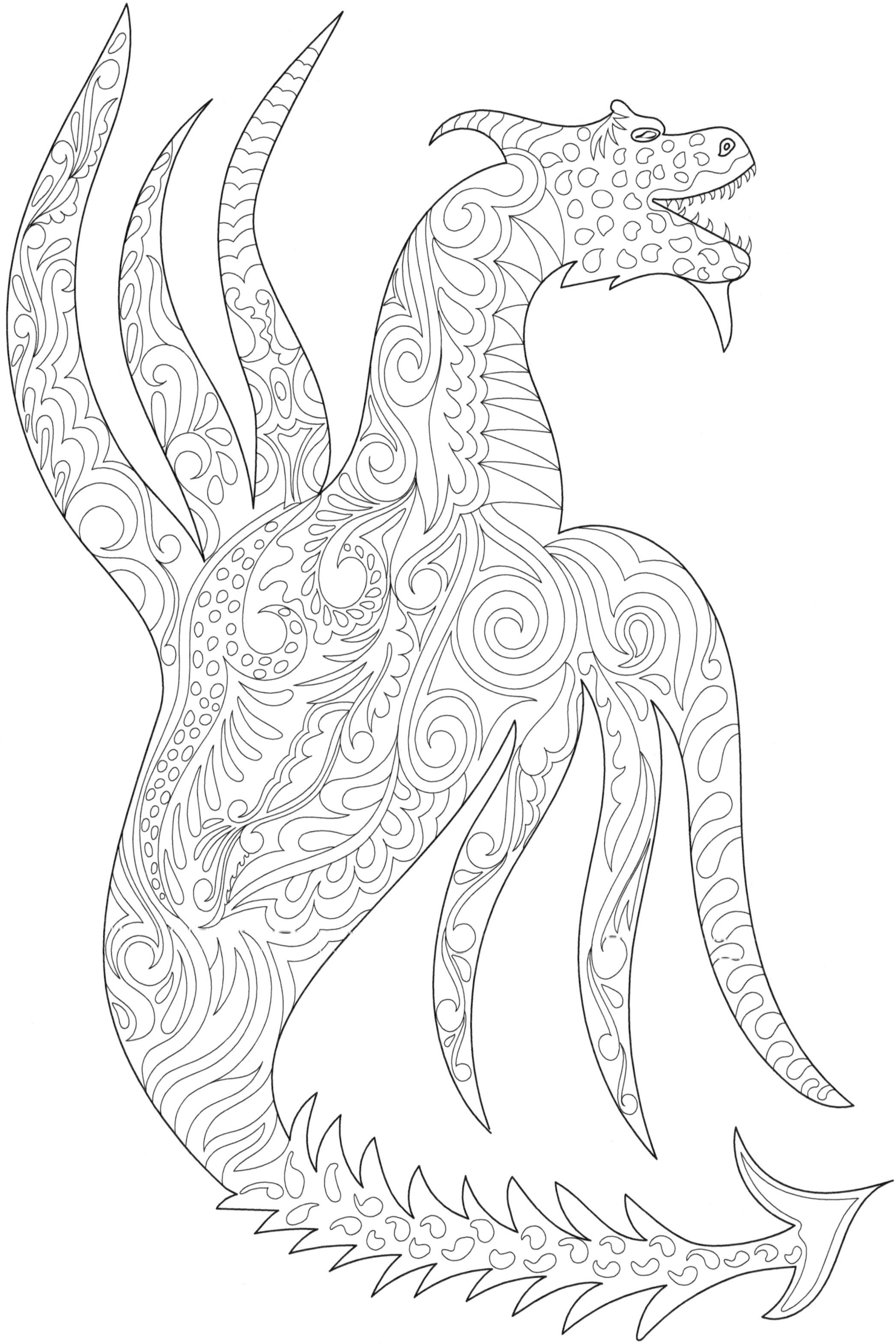

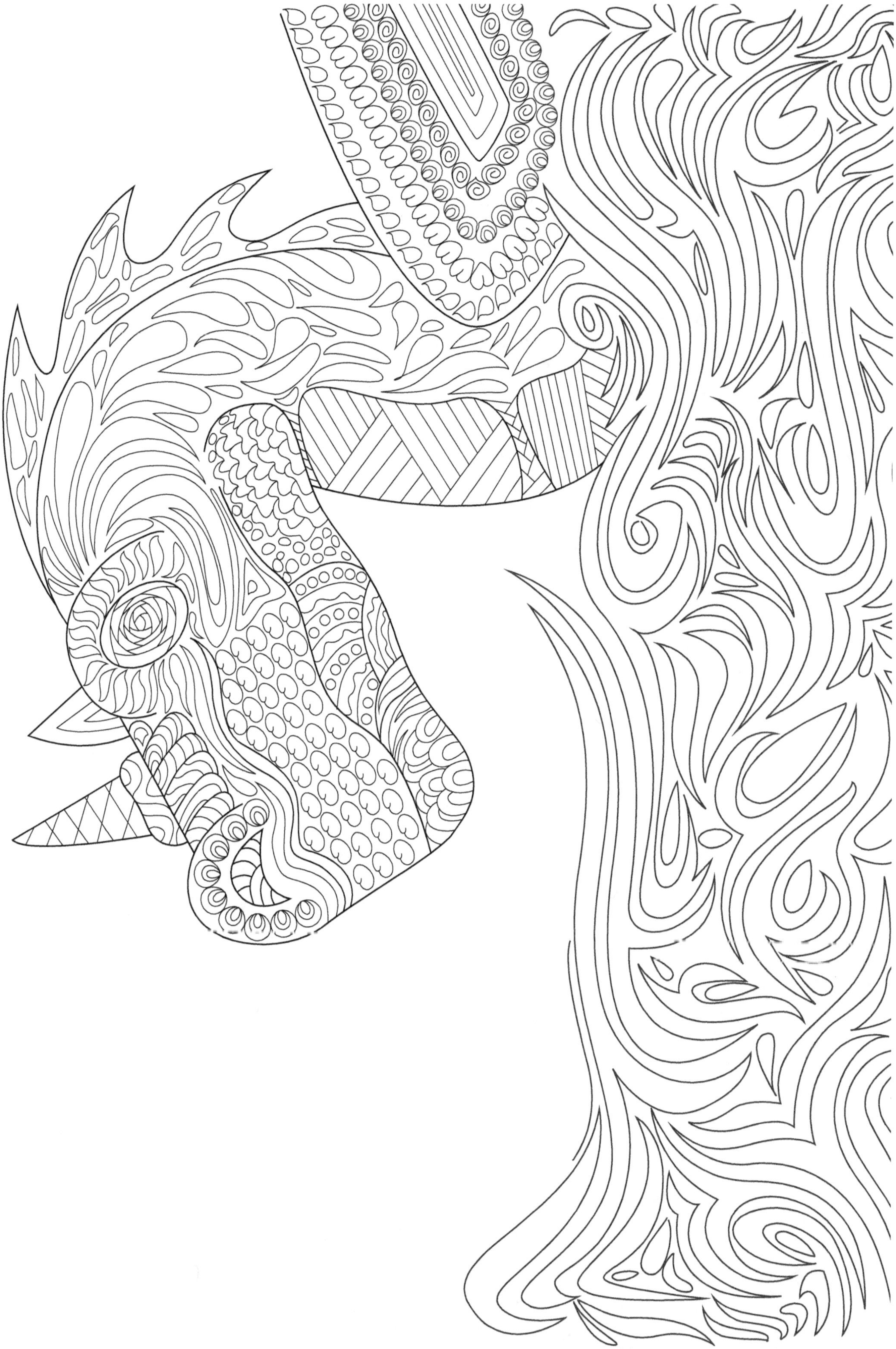

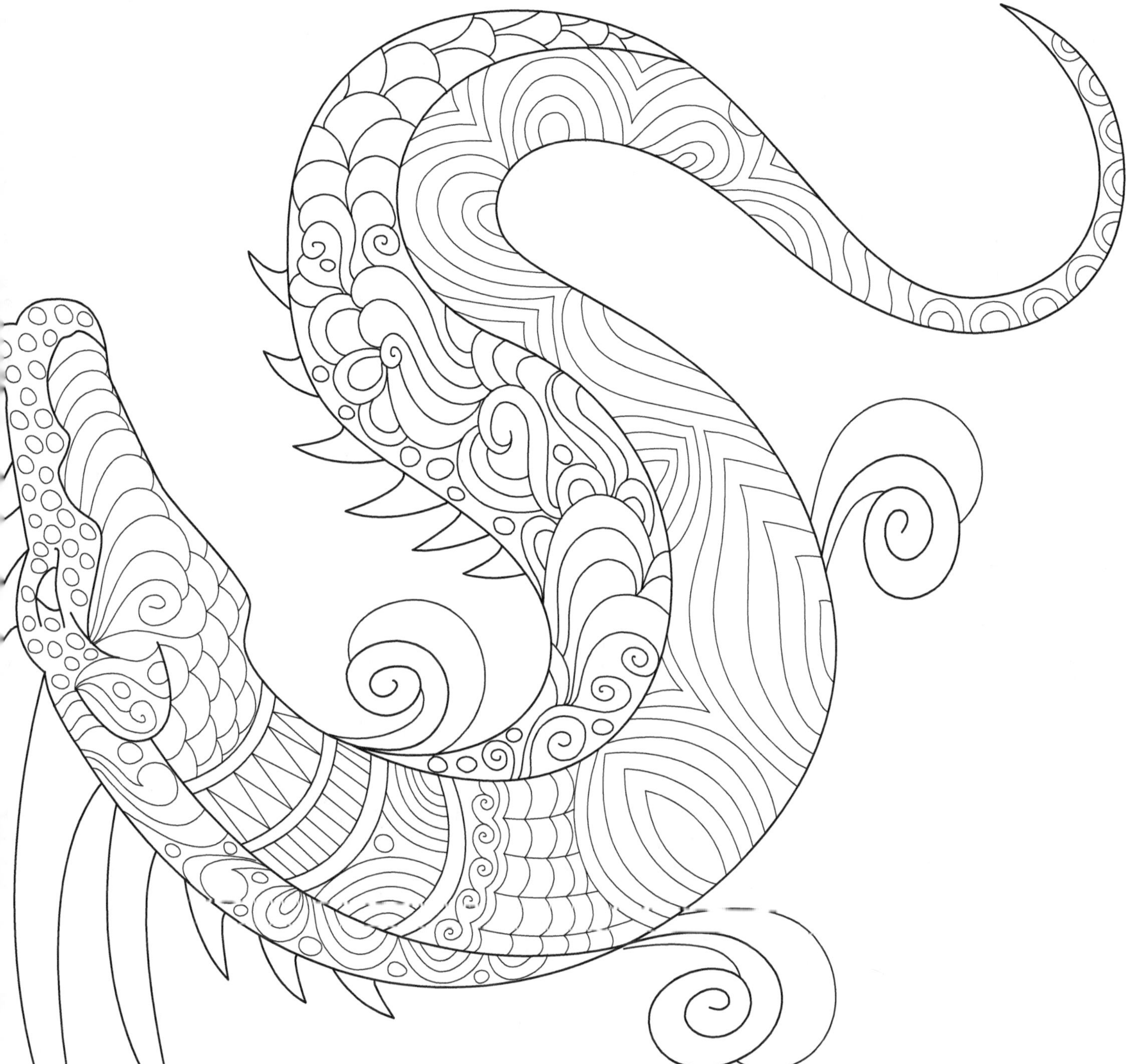

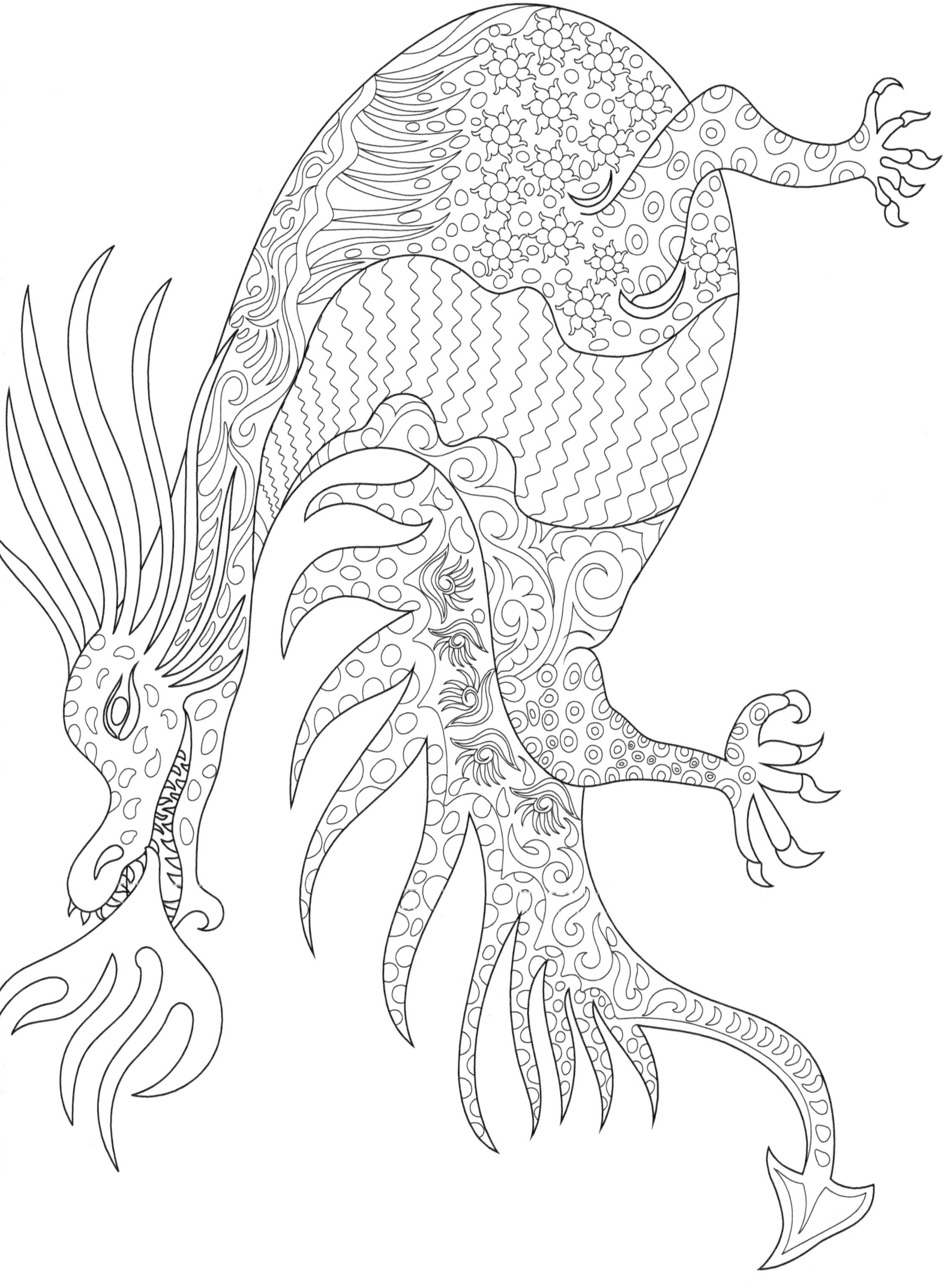

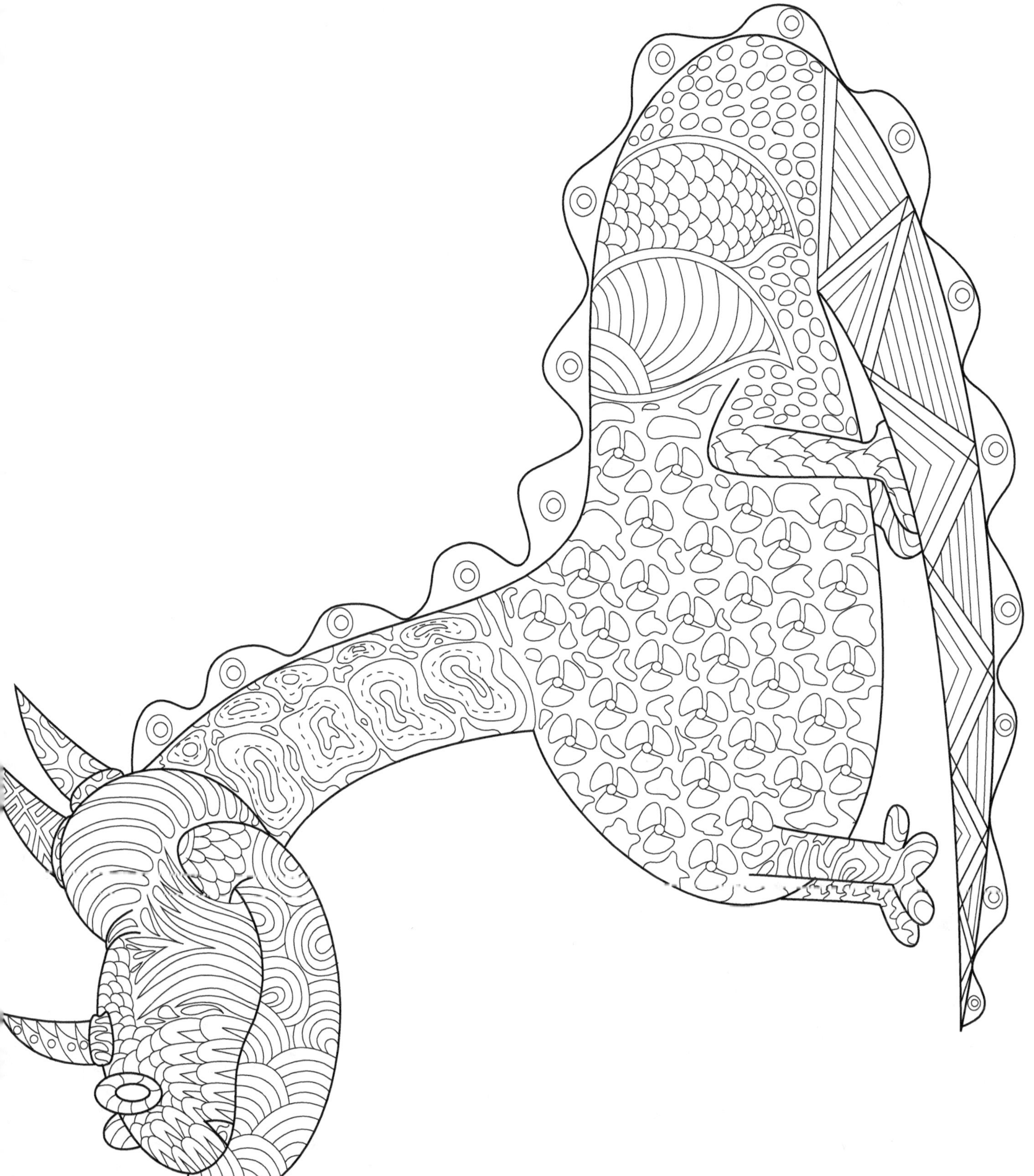

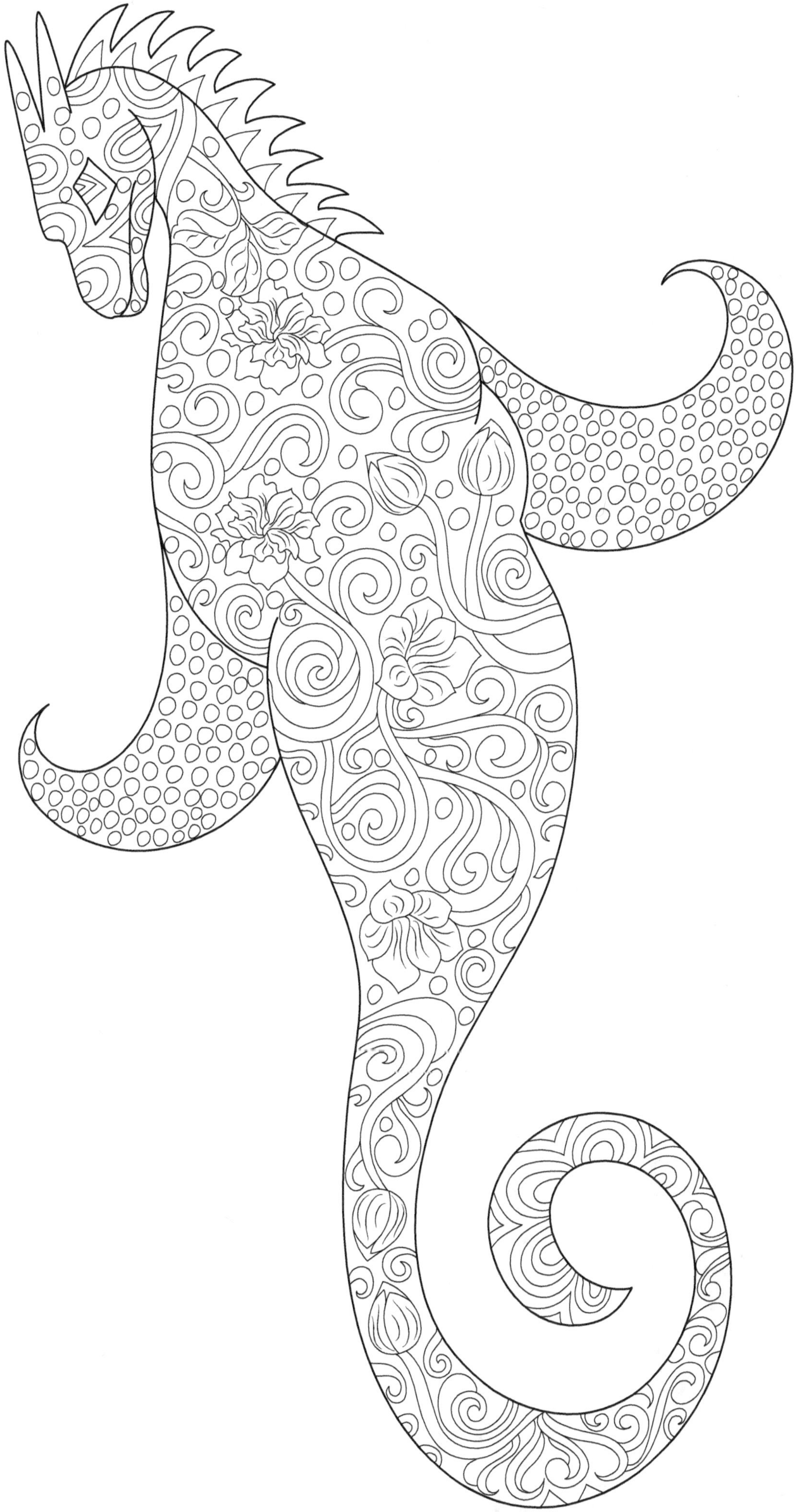

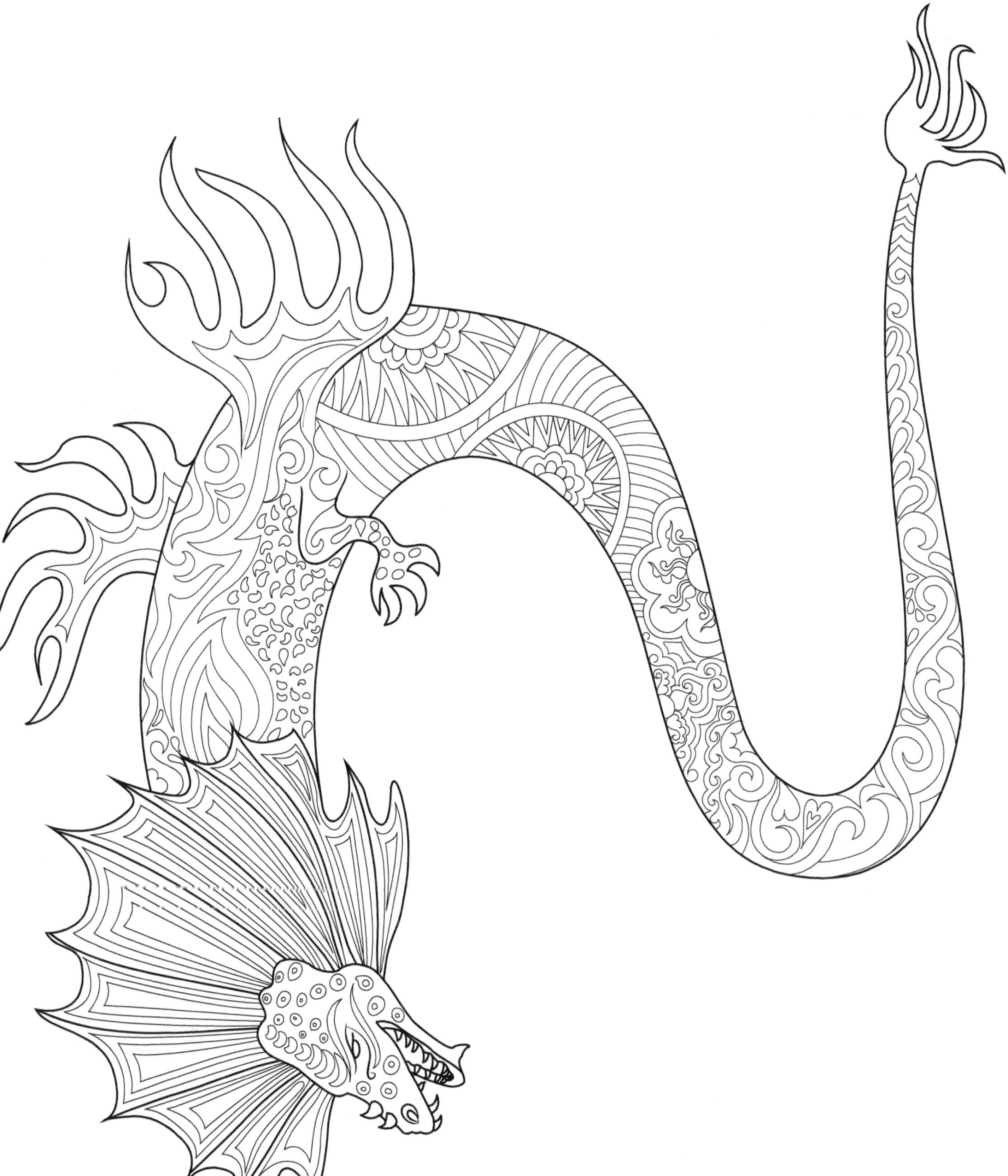

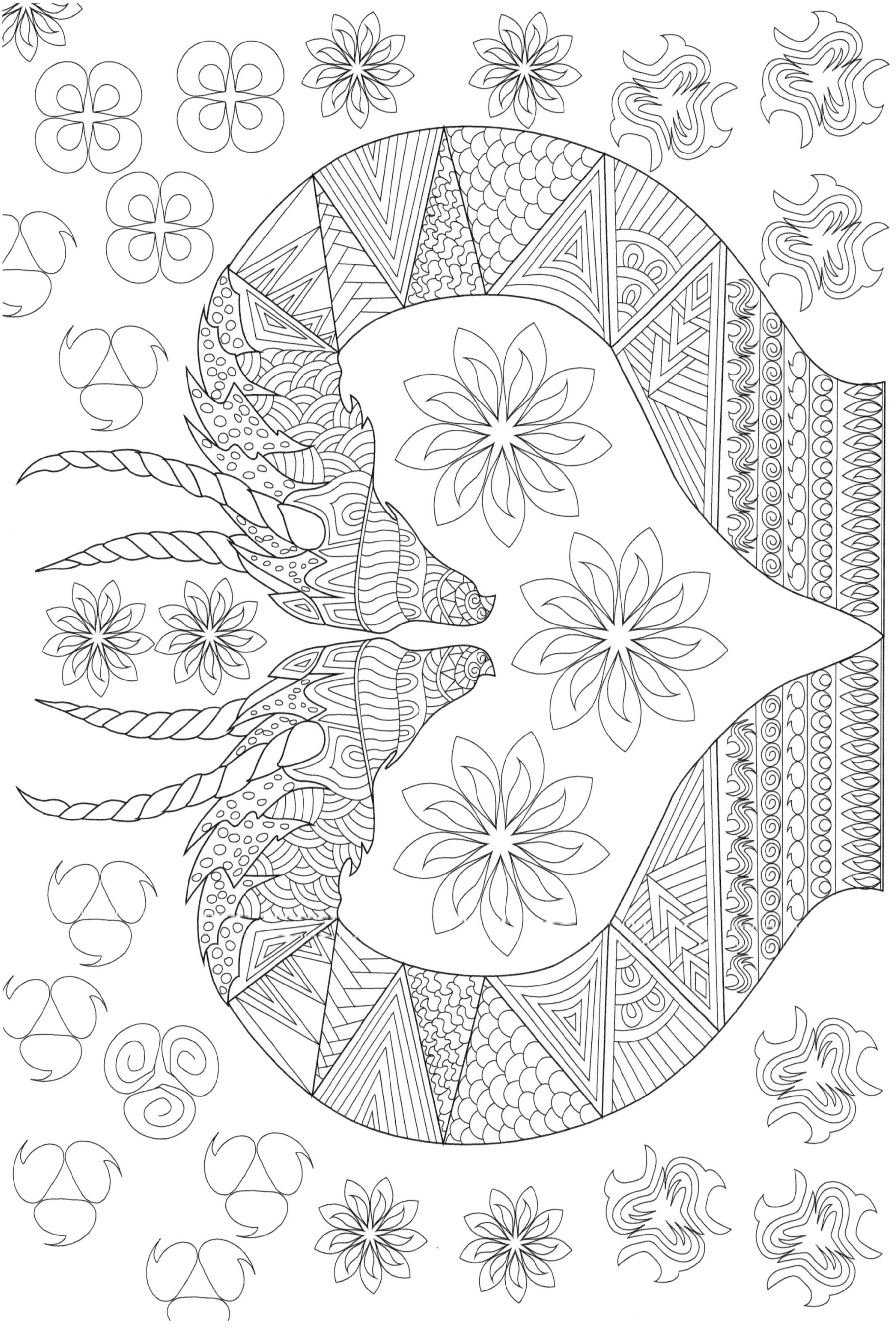

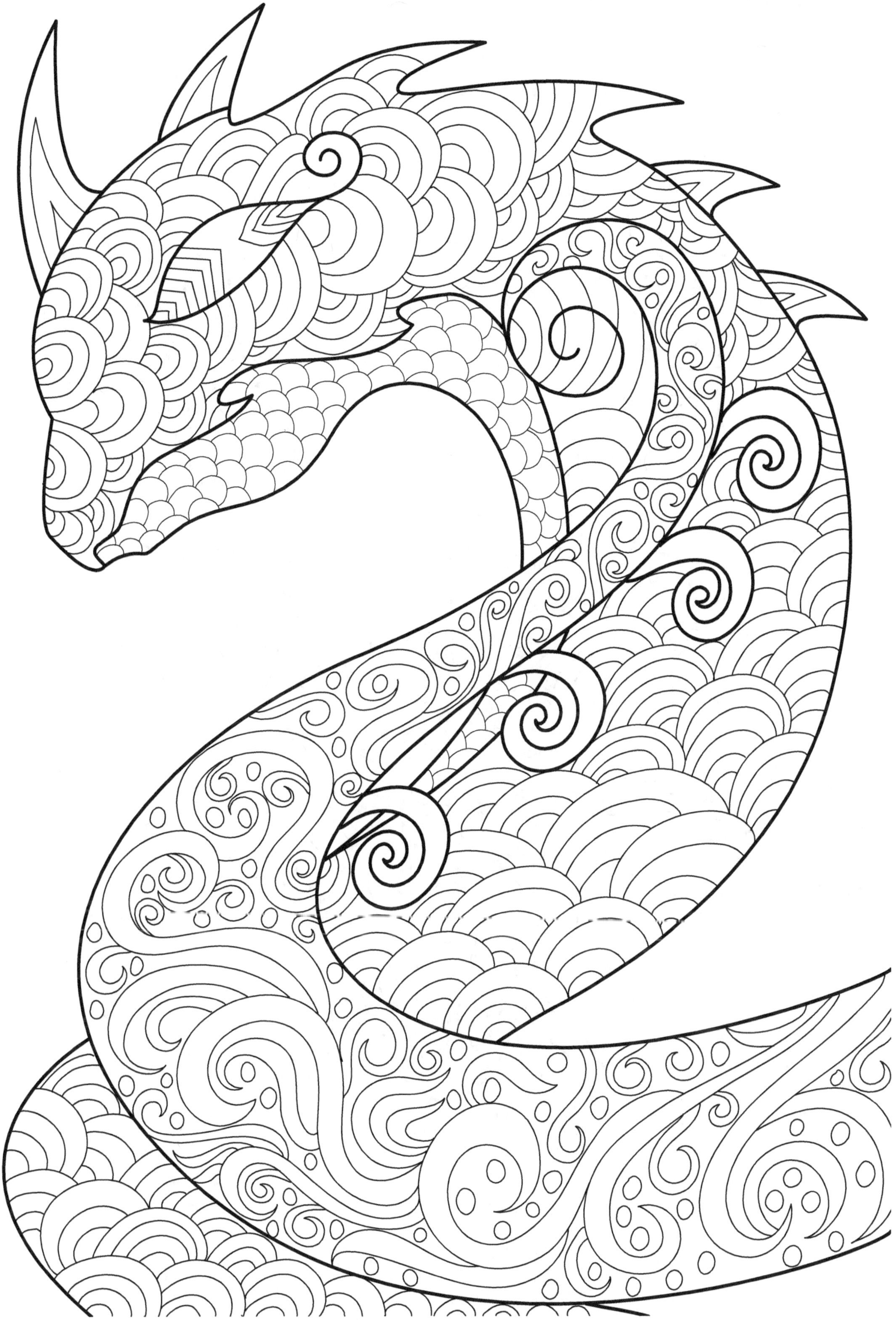

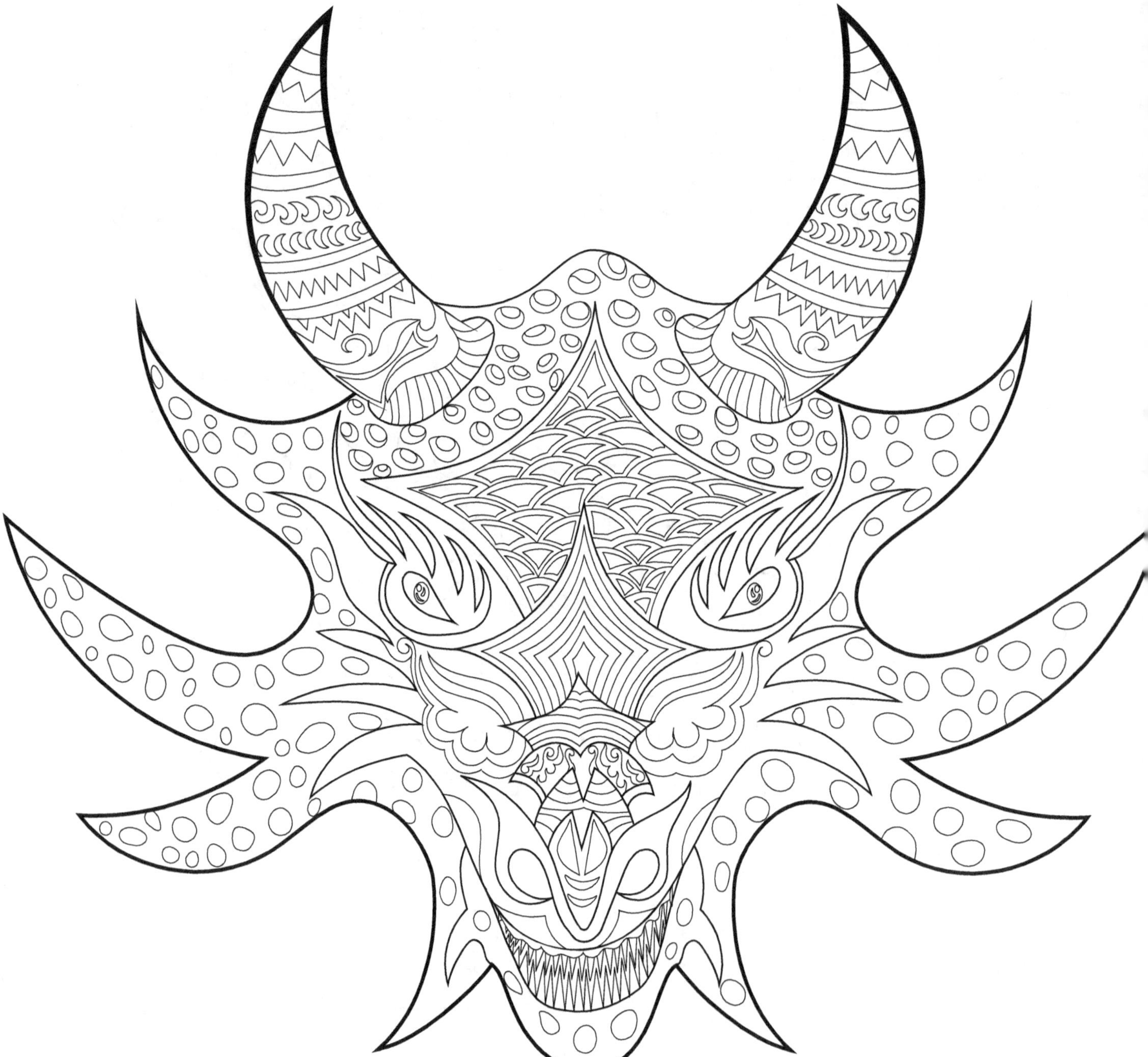

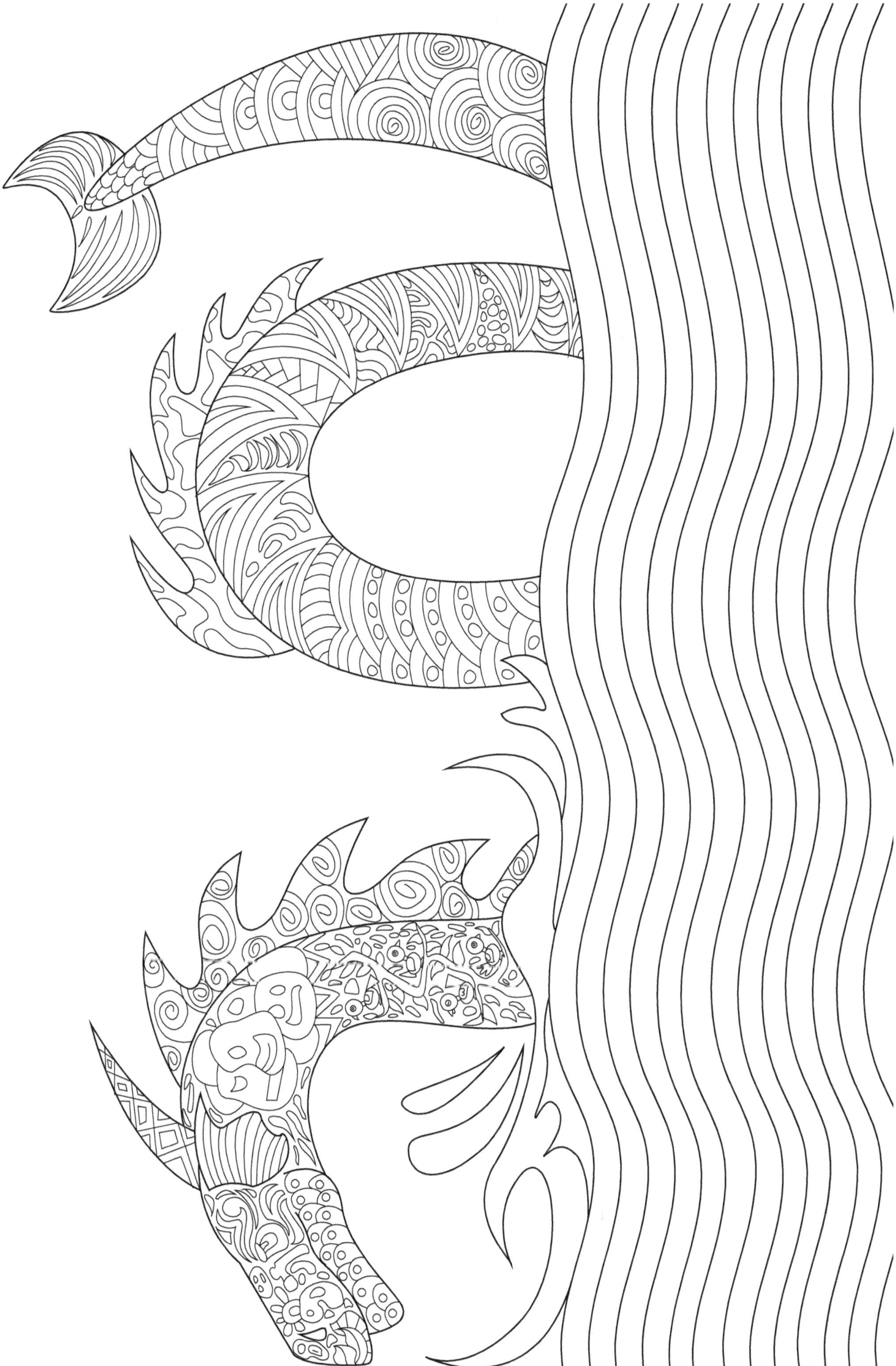

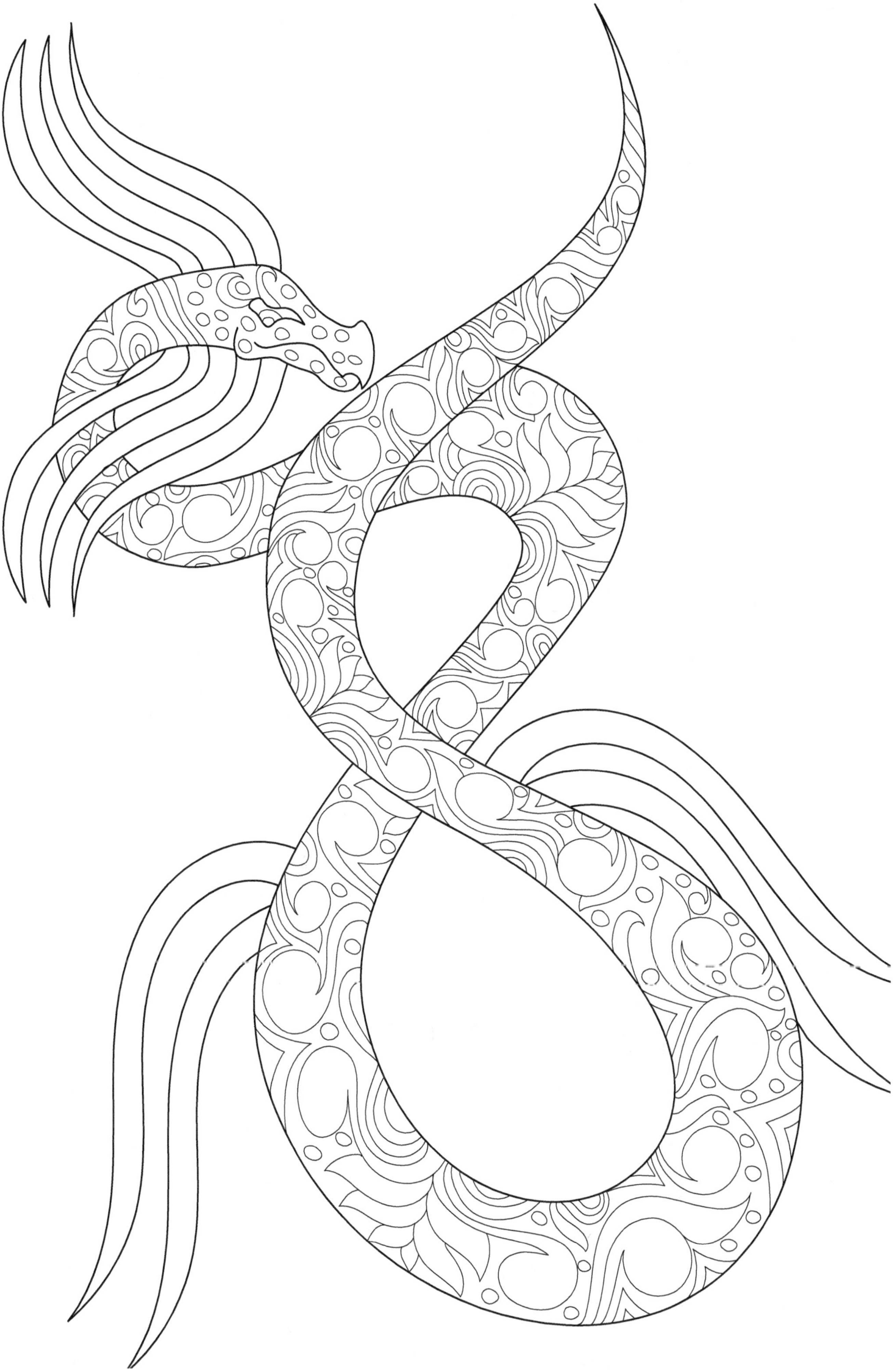

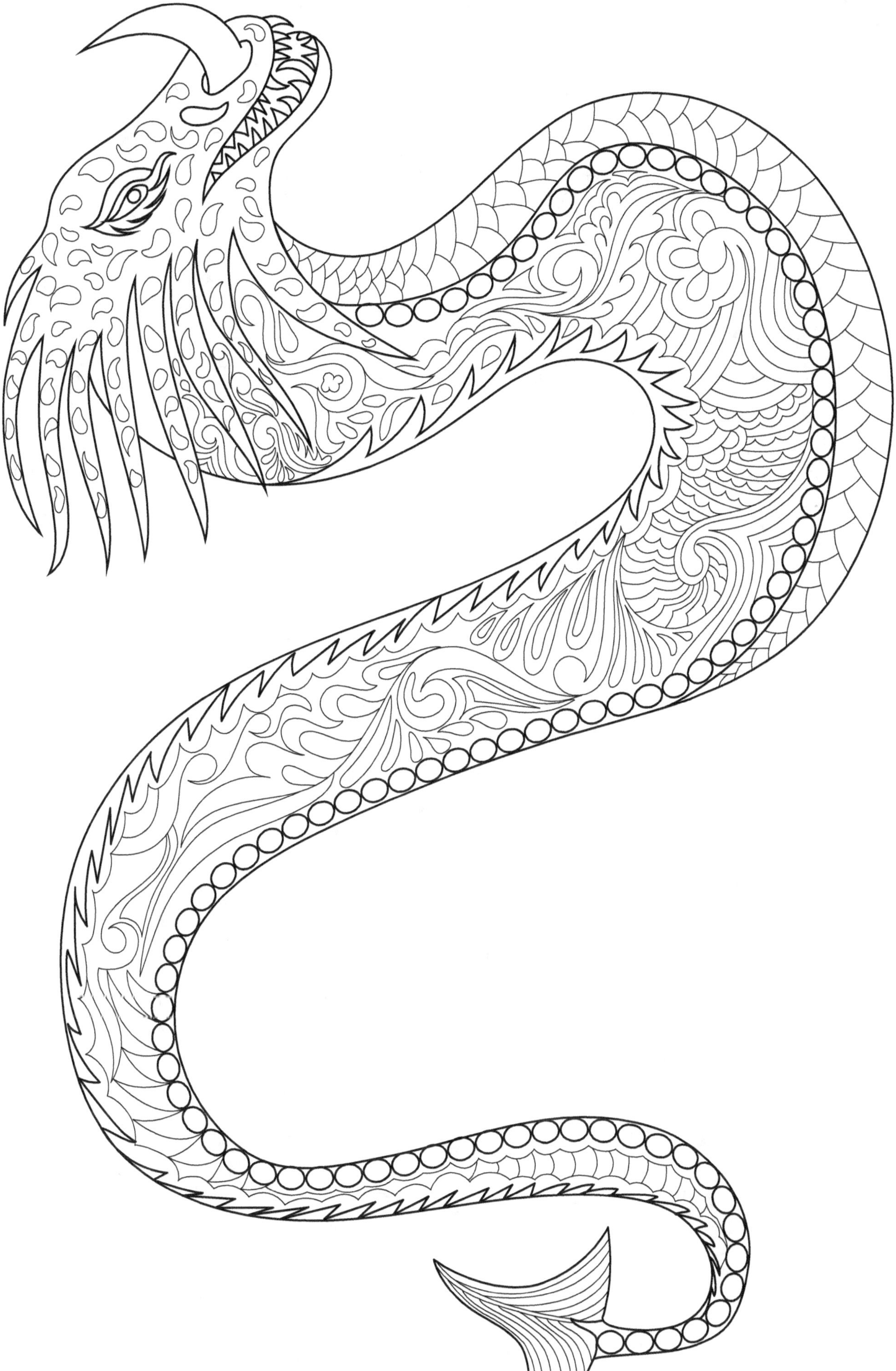

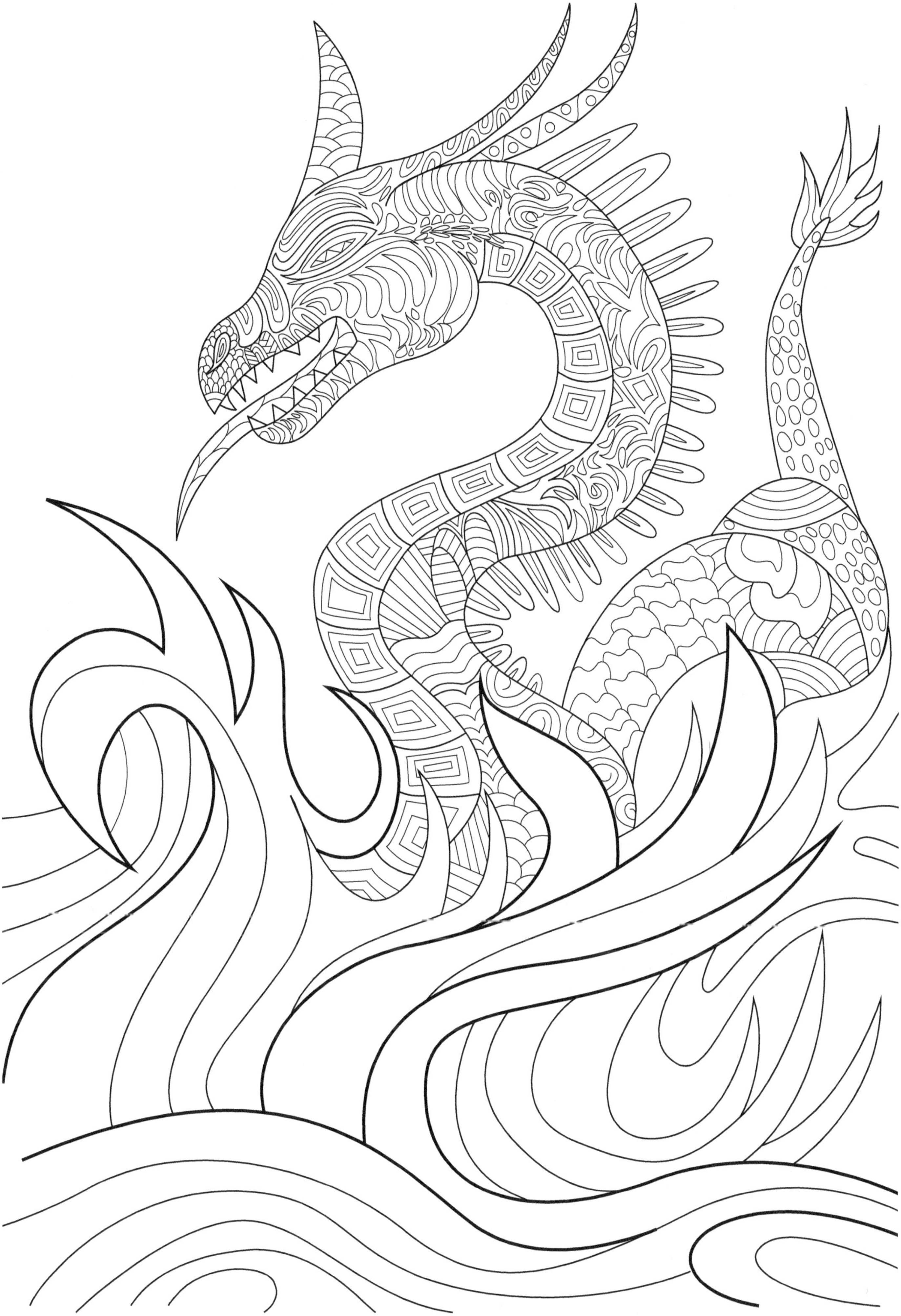

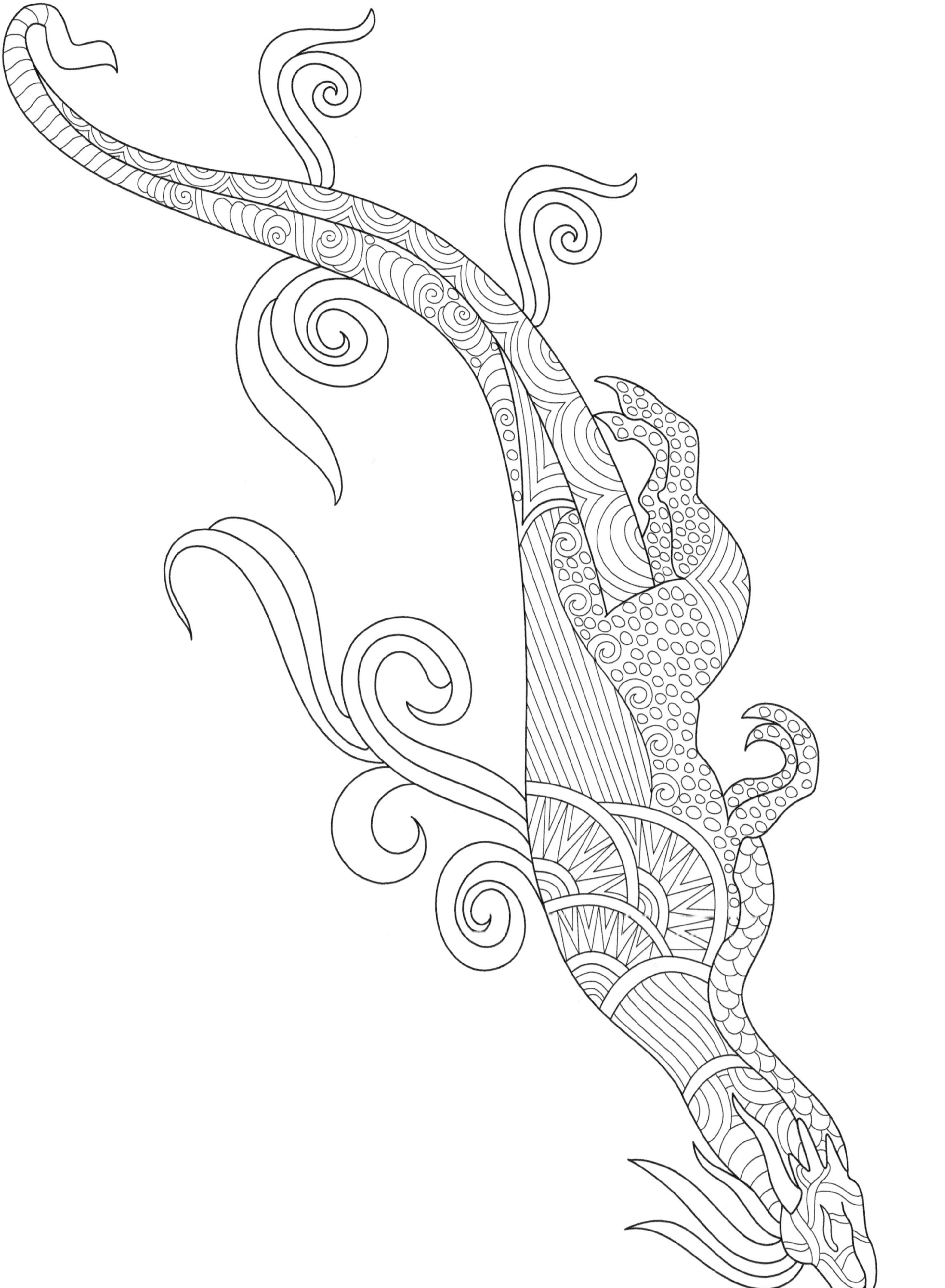

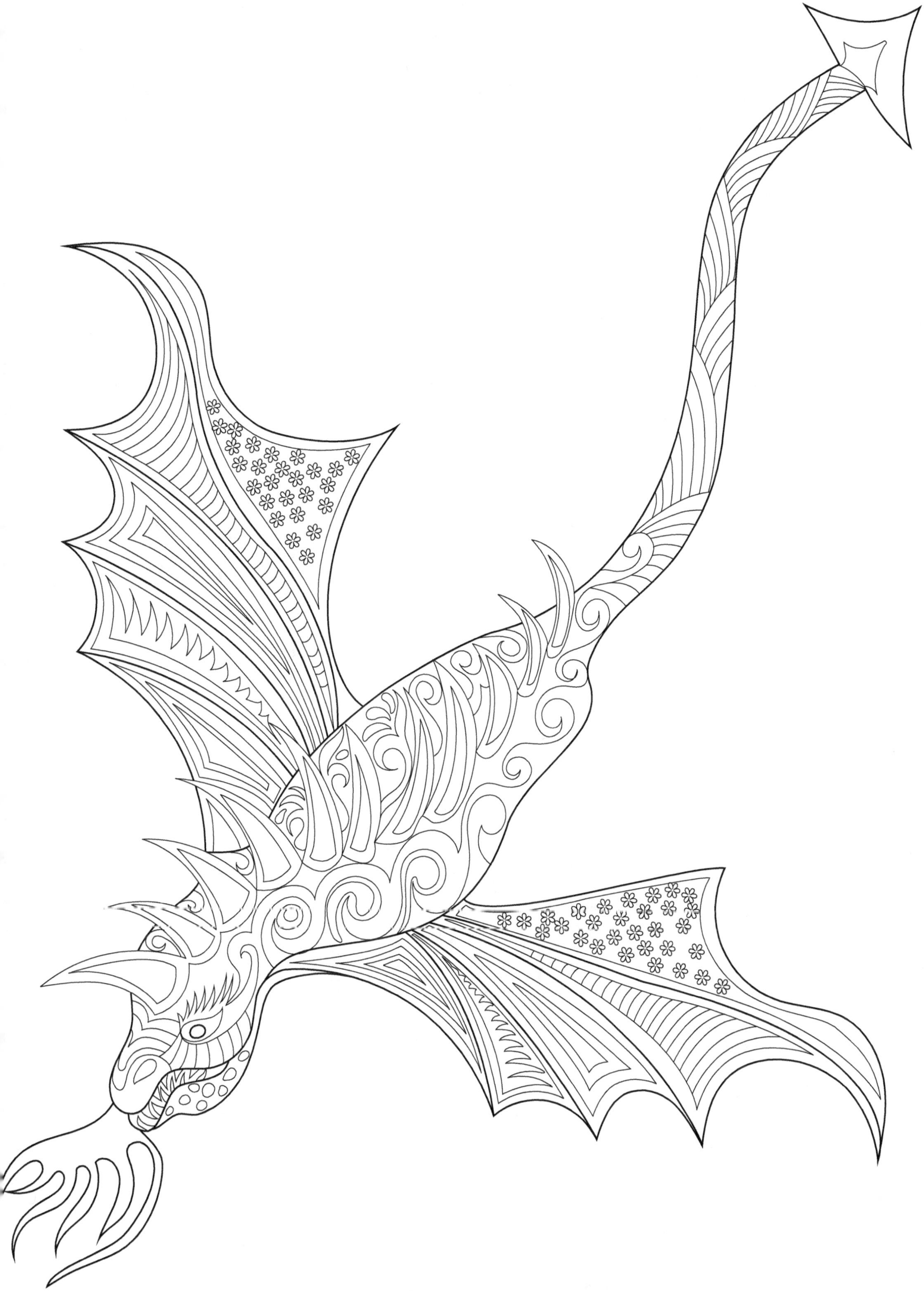

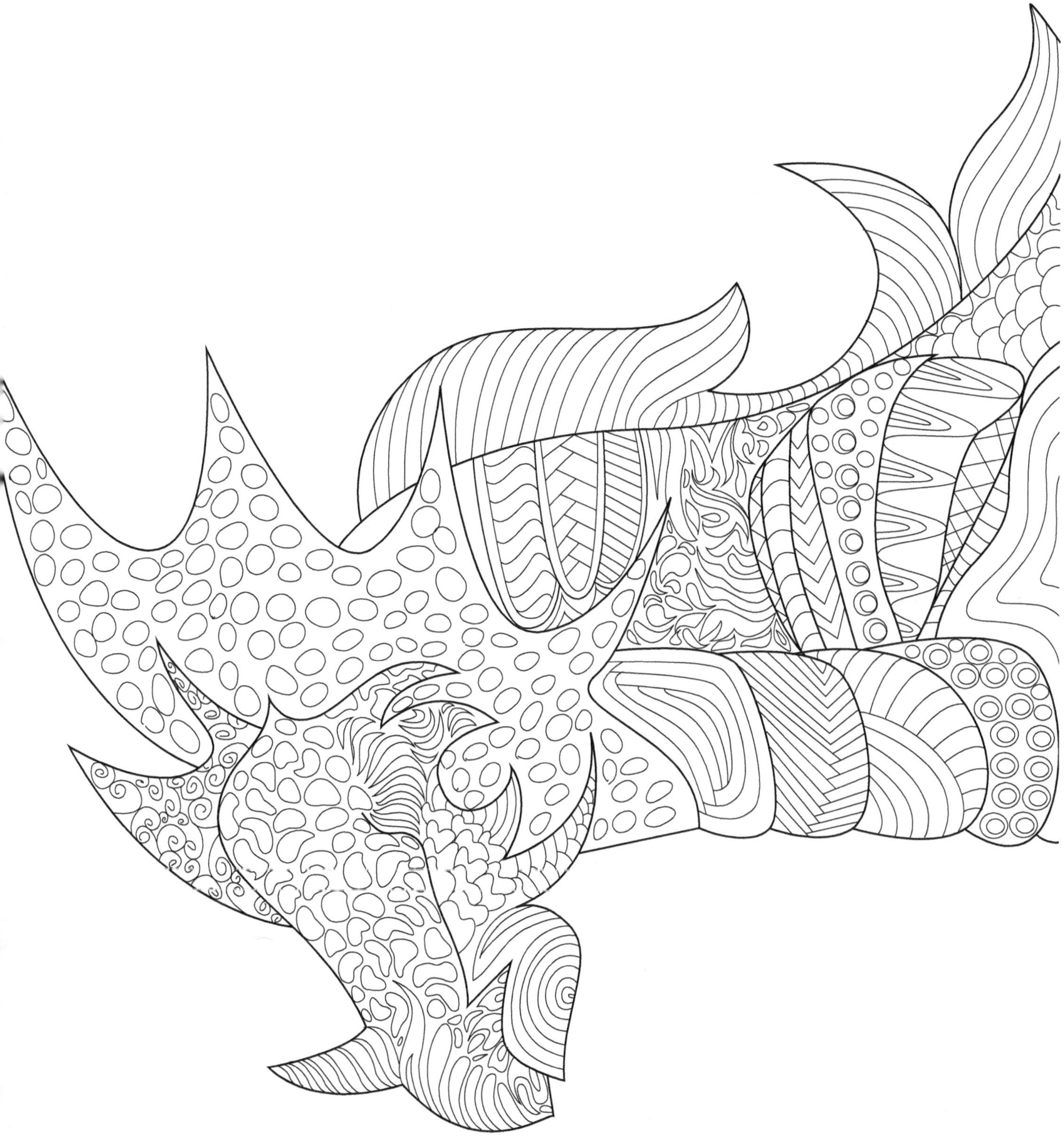

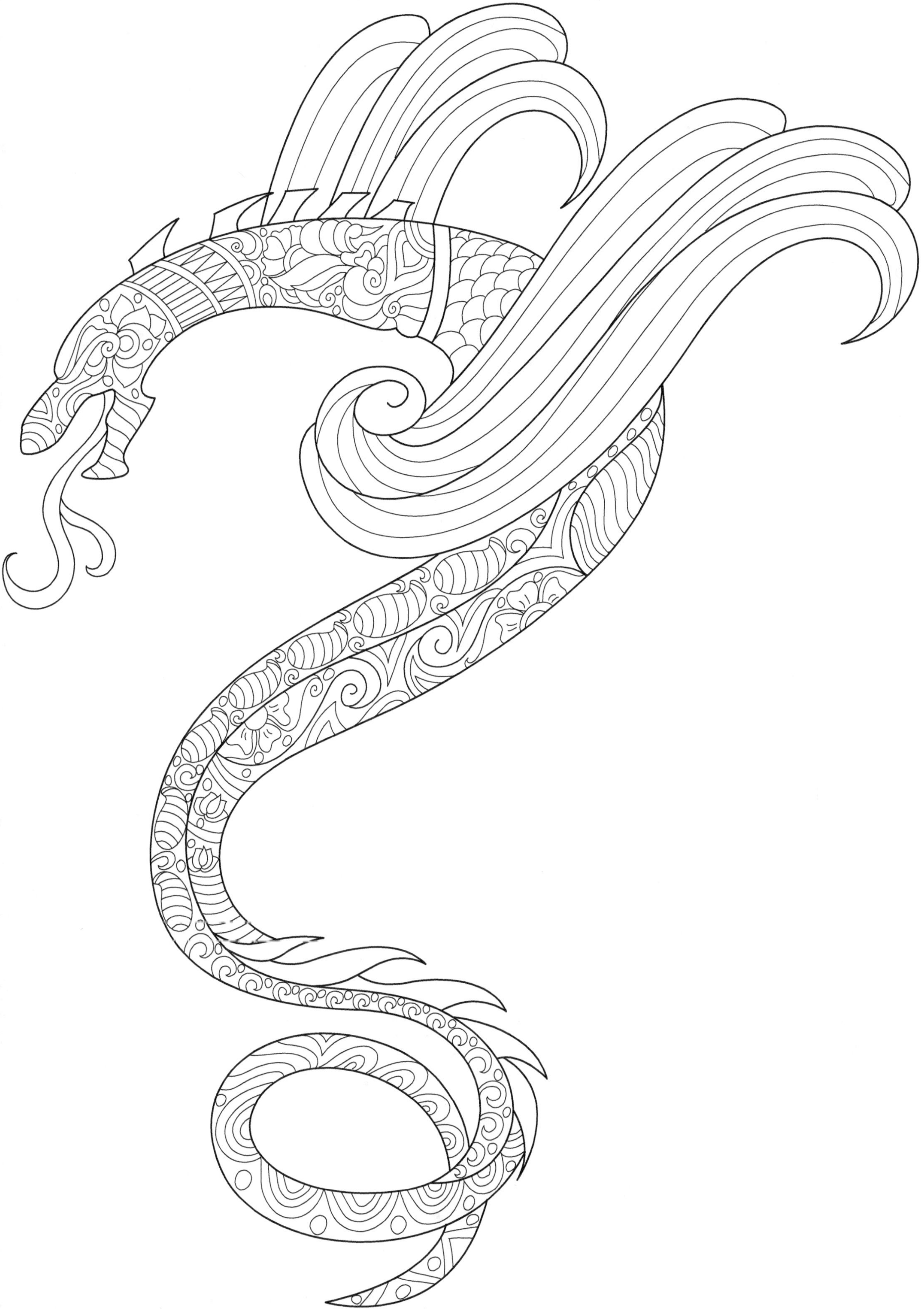

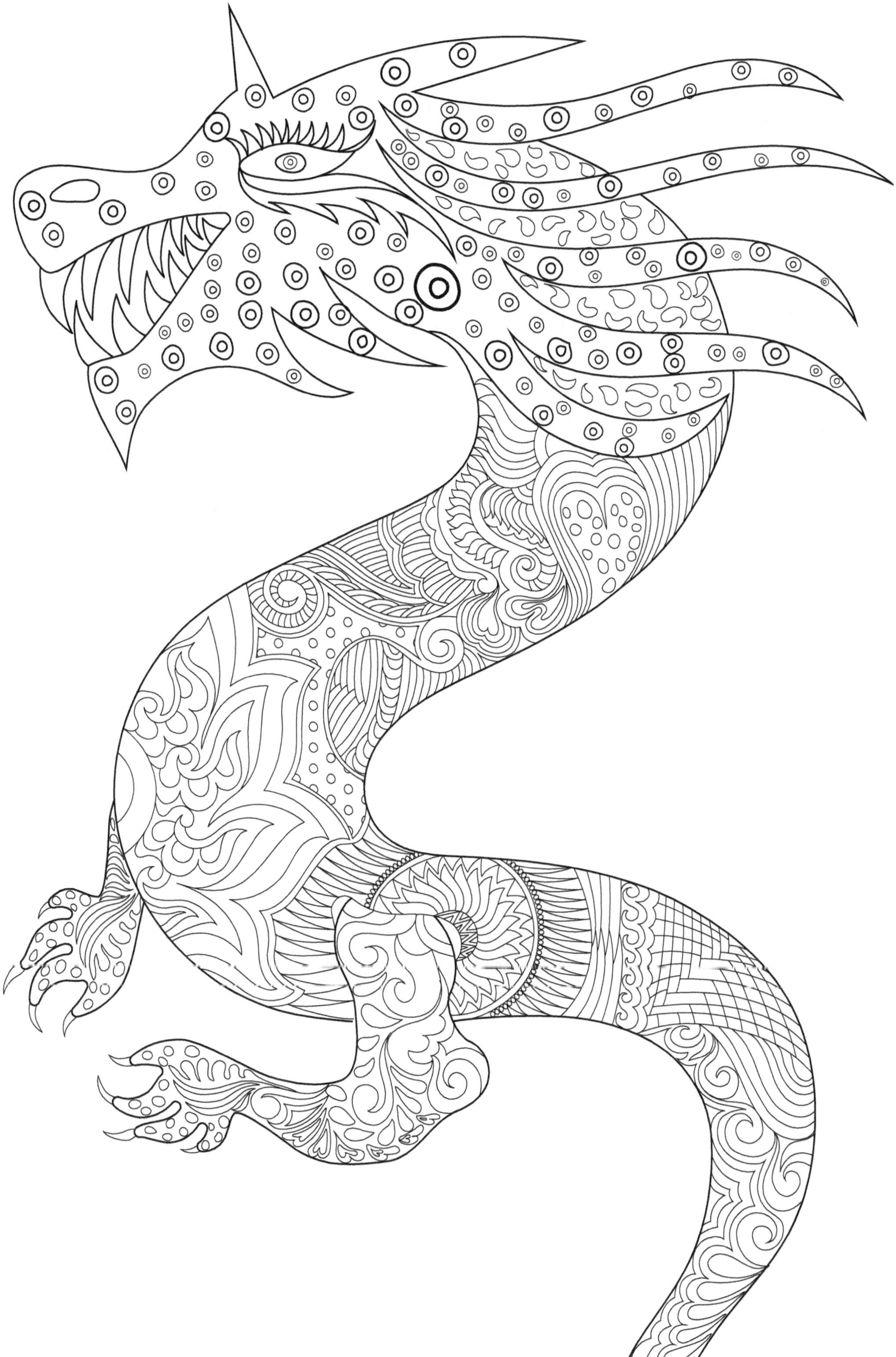

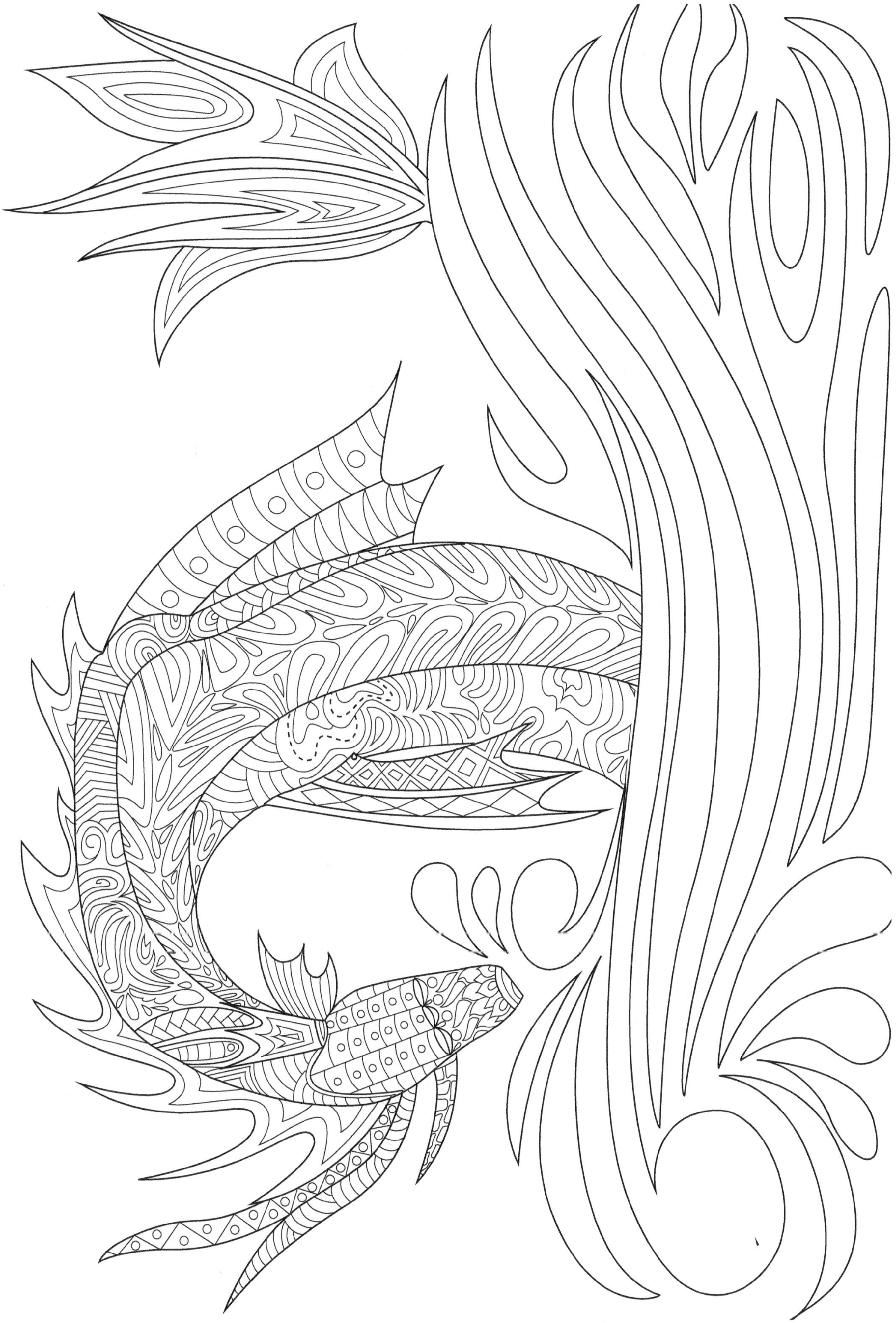

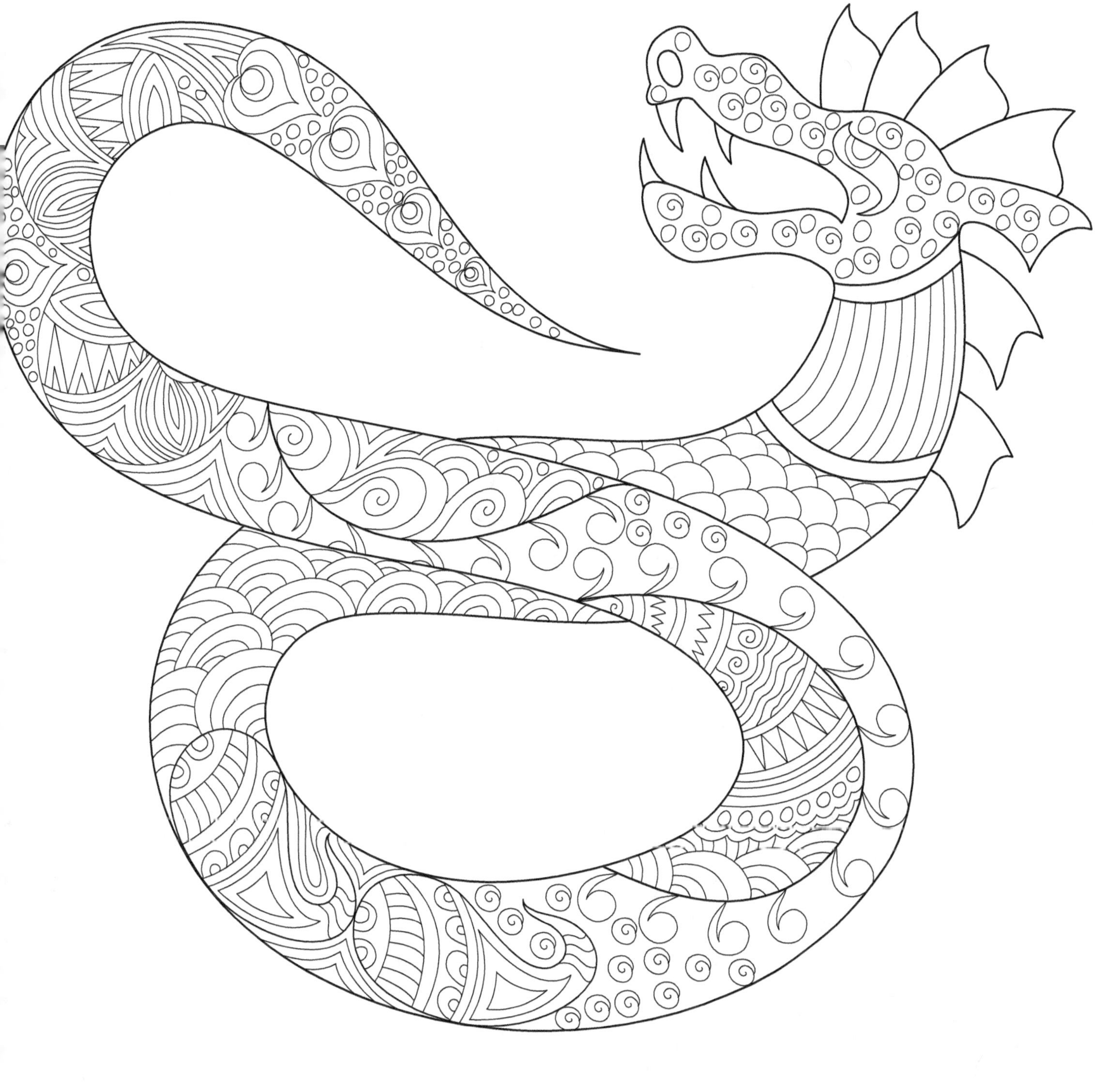

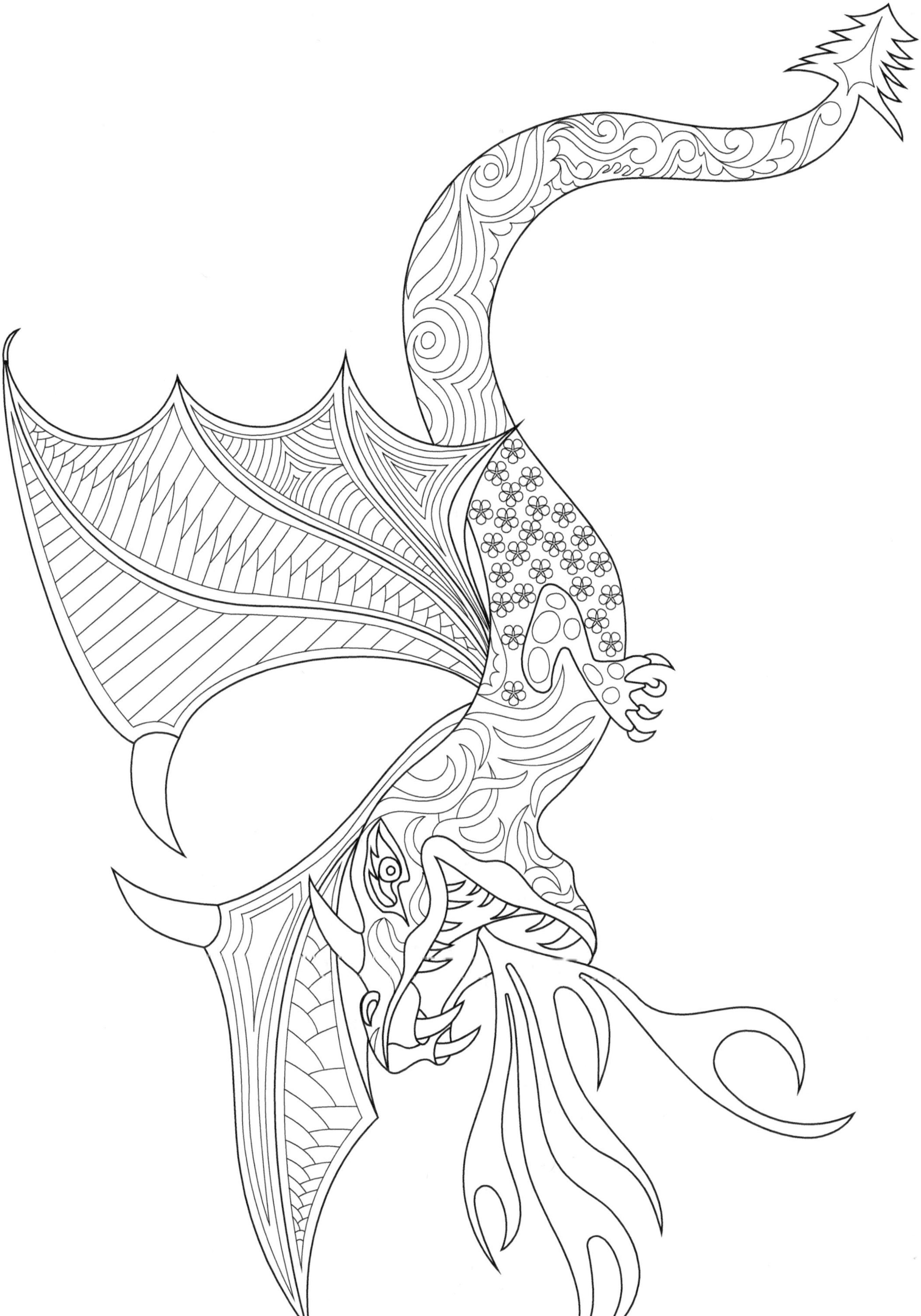

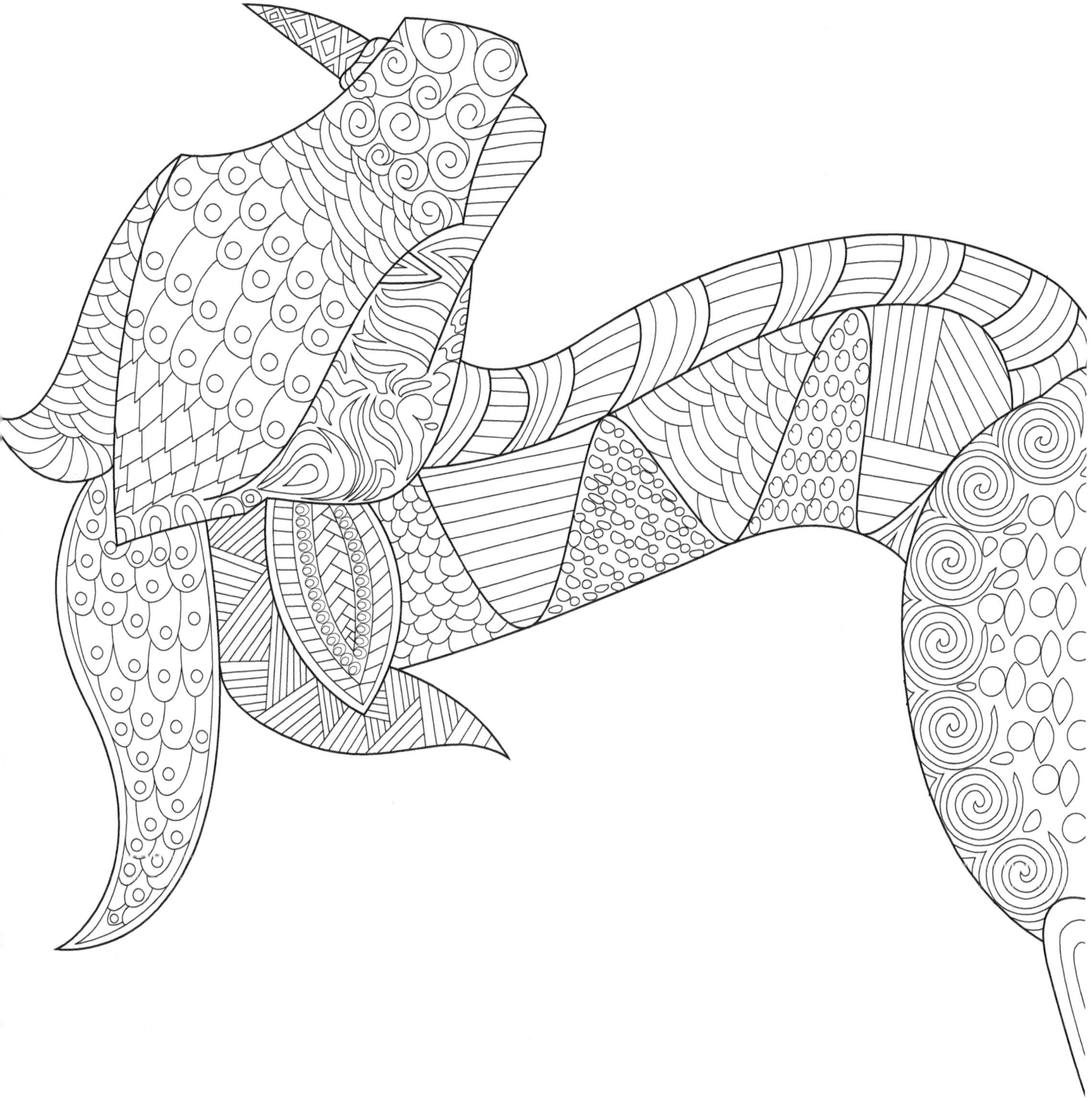

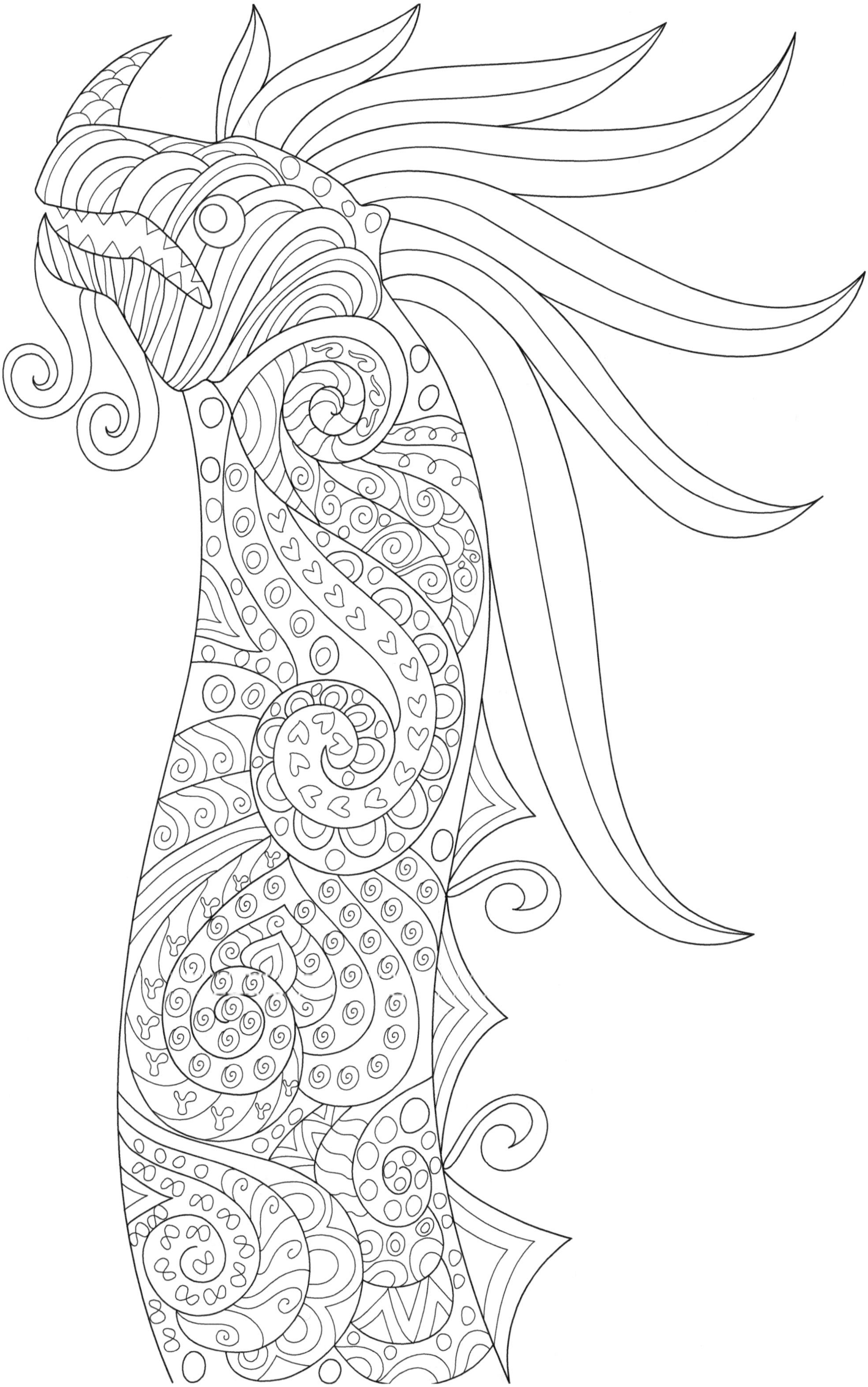

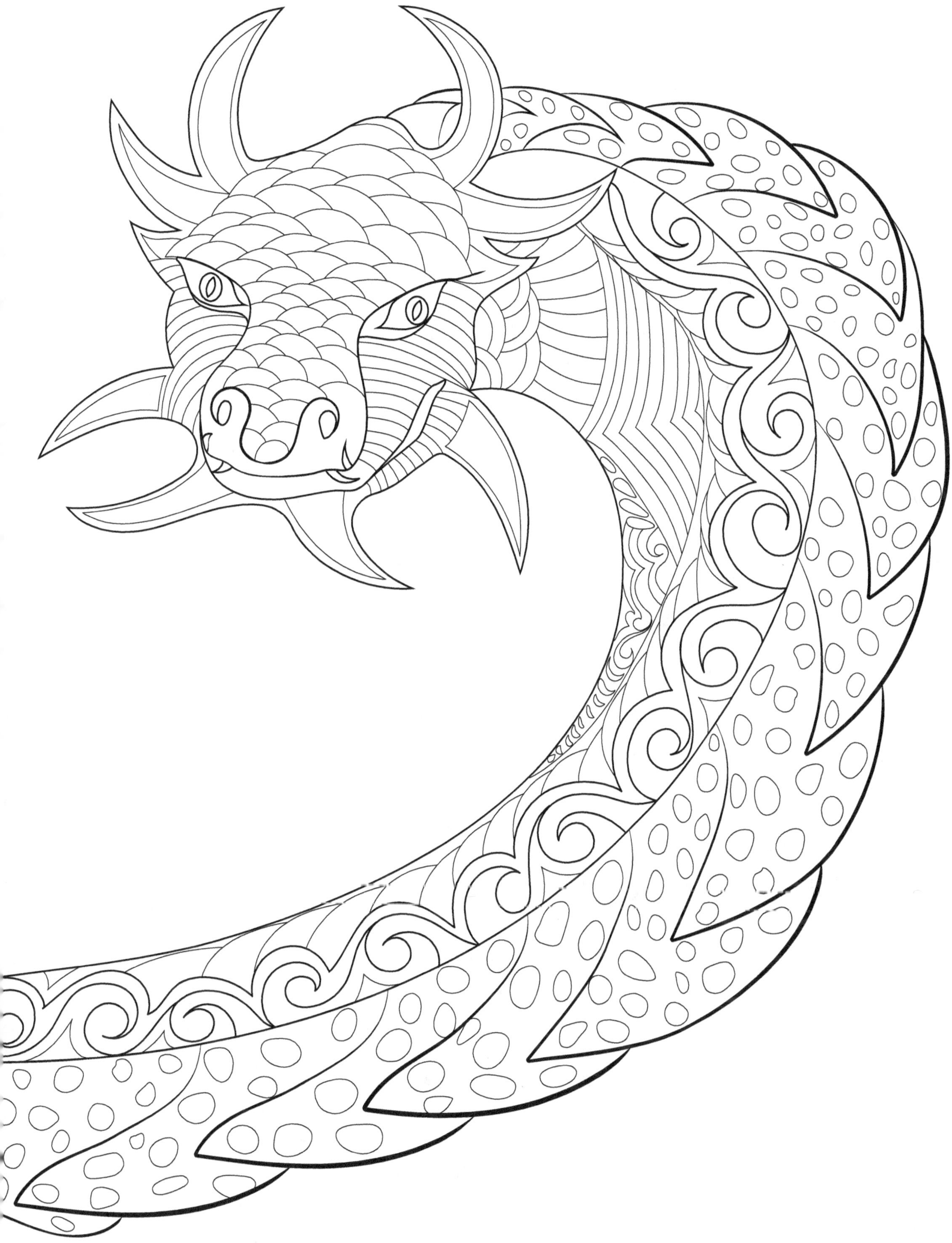

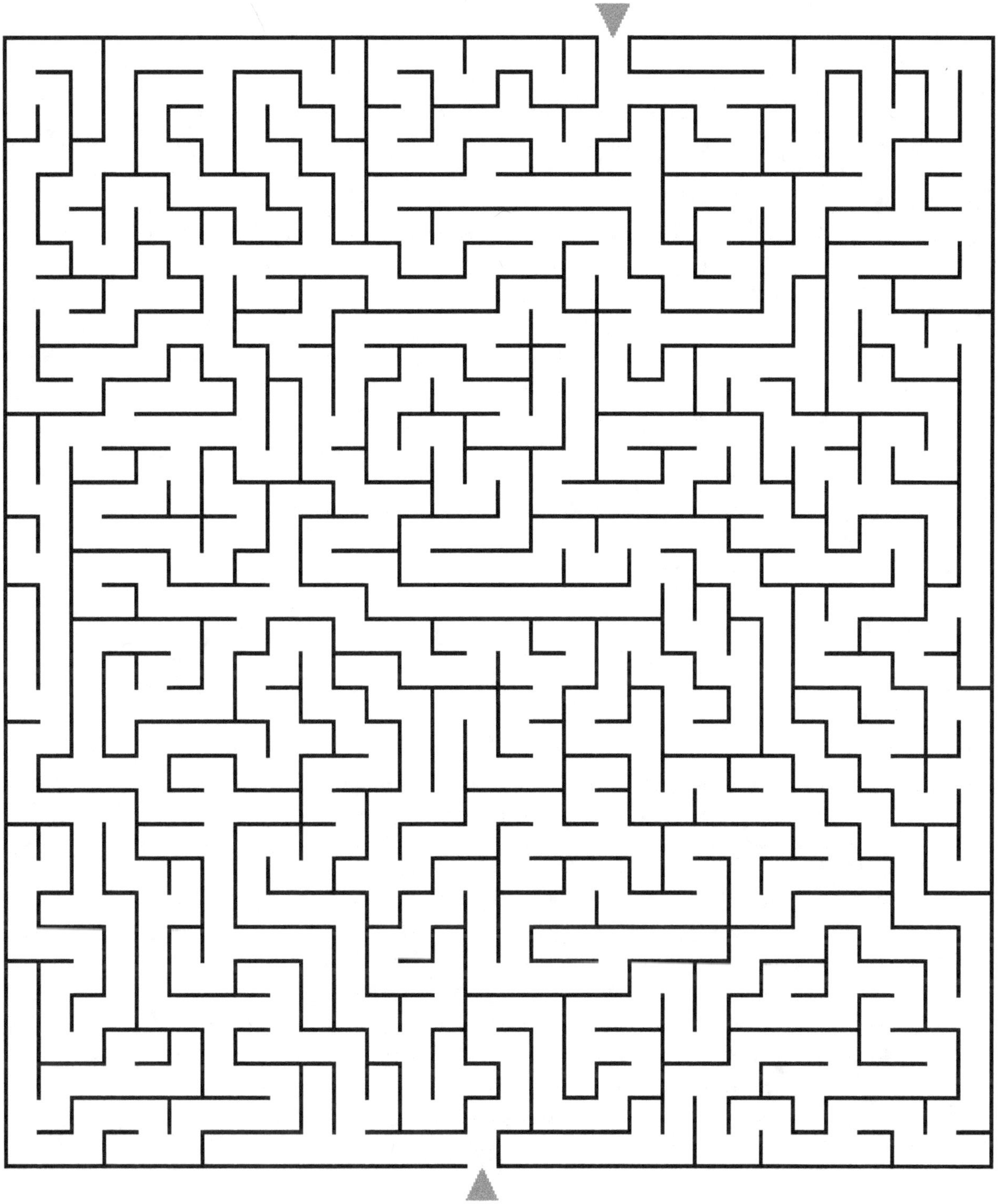

COLOR CHARTS

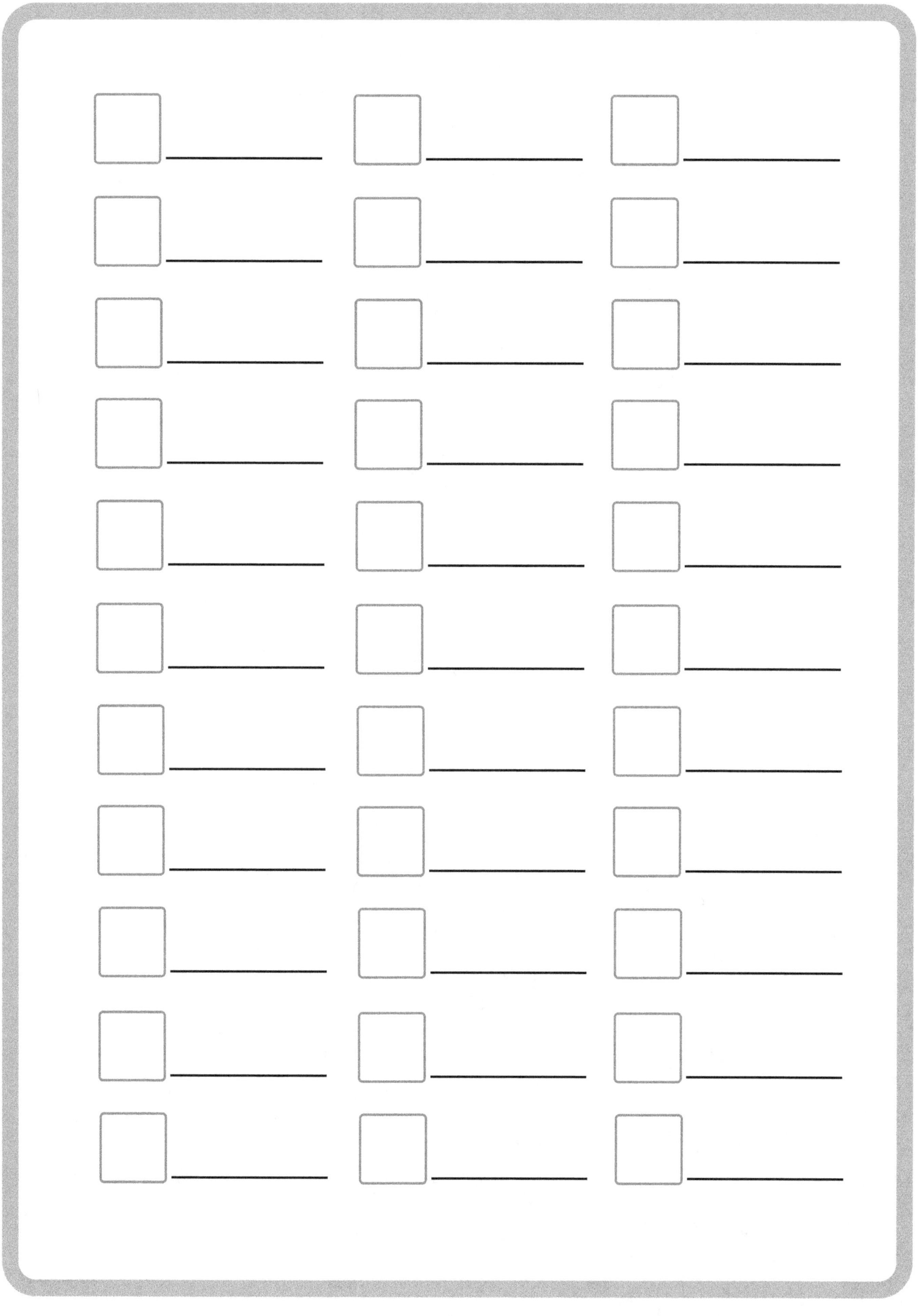

Solution

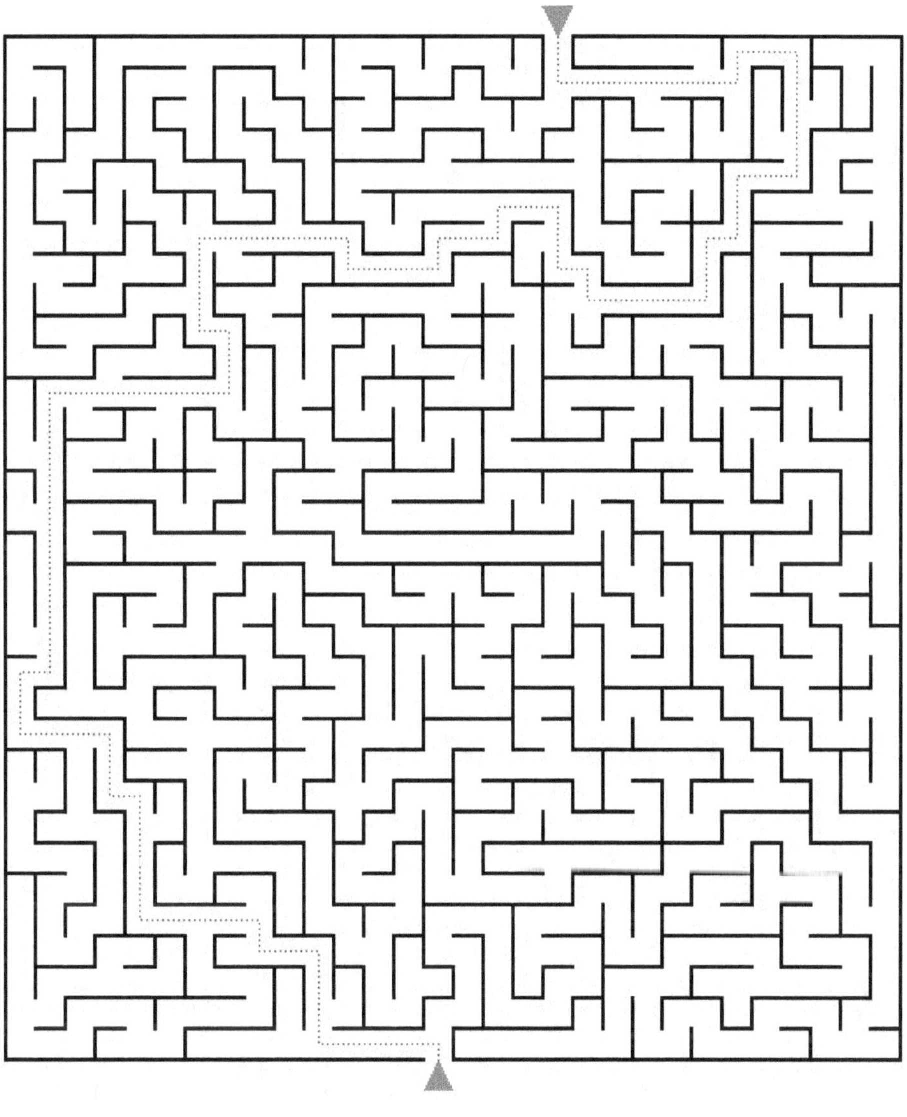

COLOR CHARTS

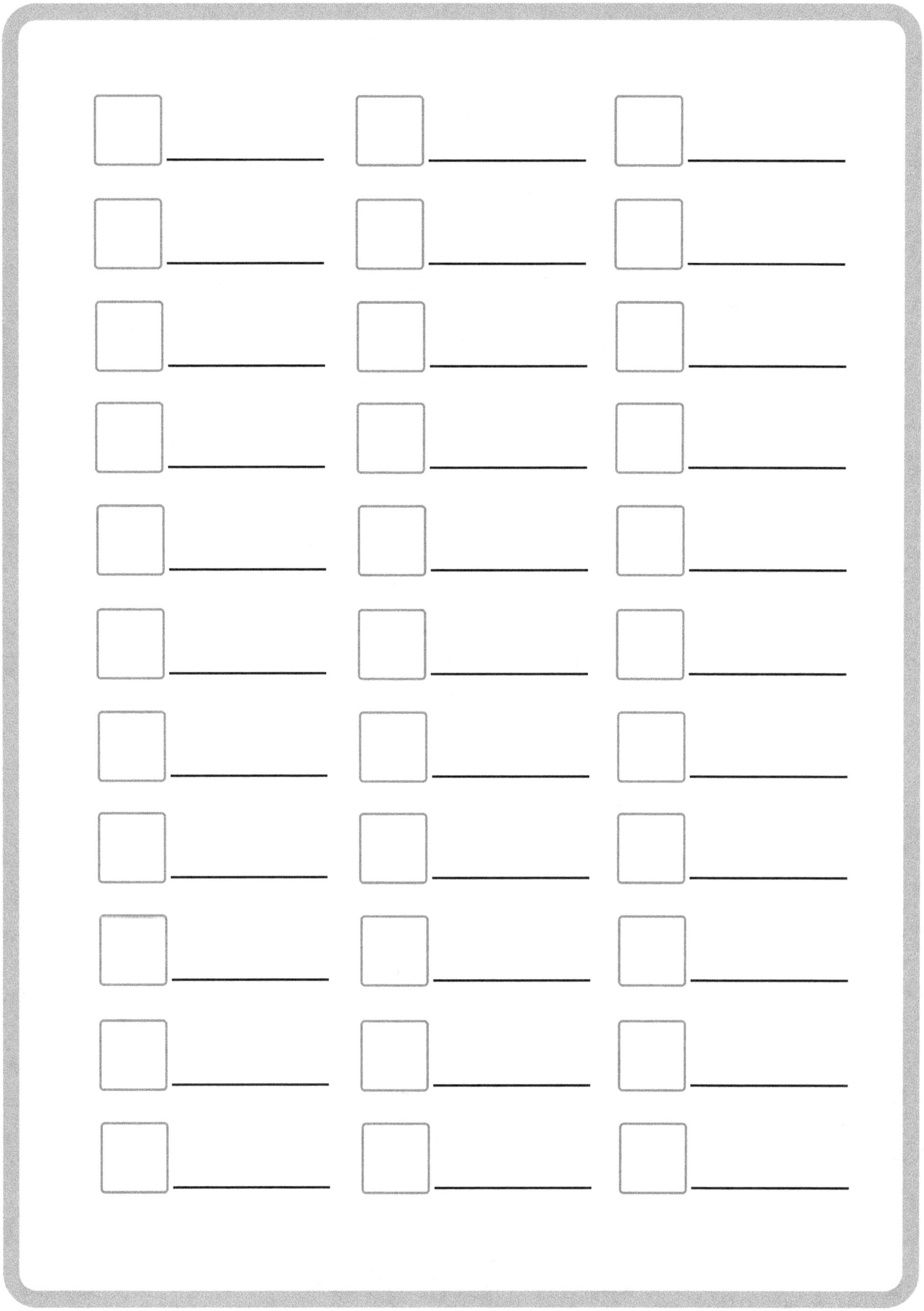

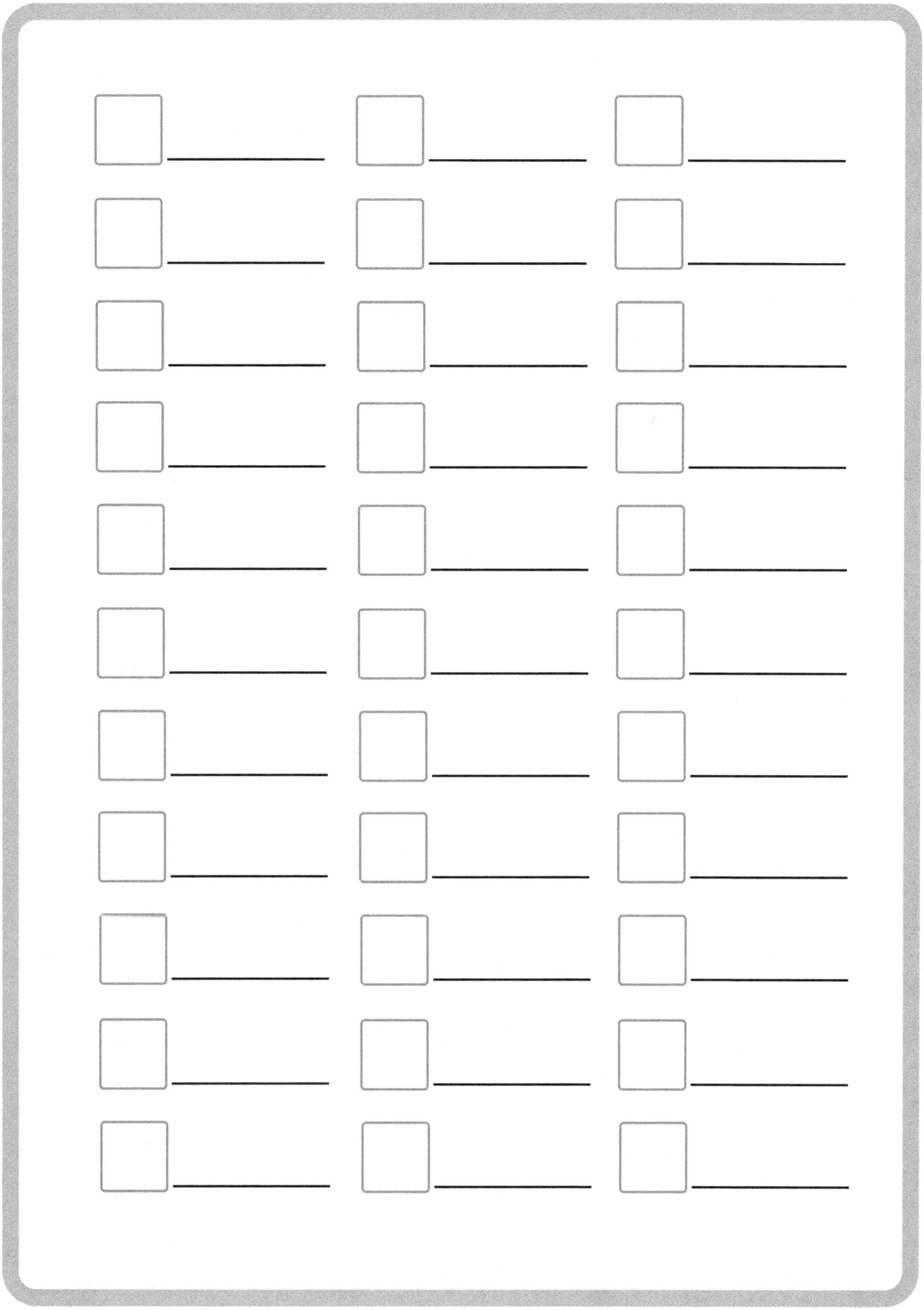

Solution

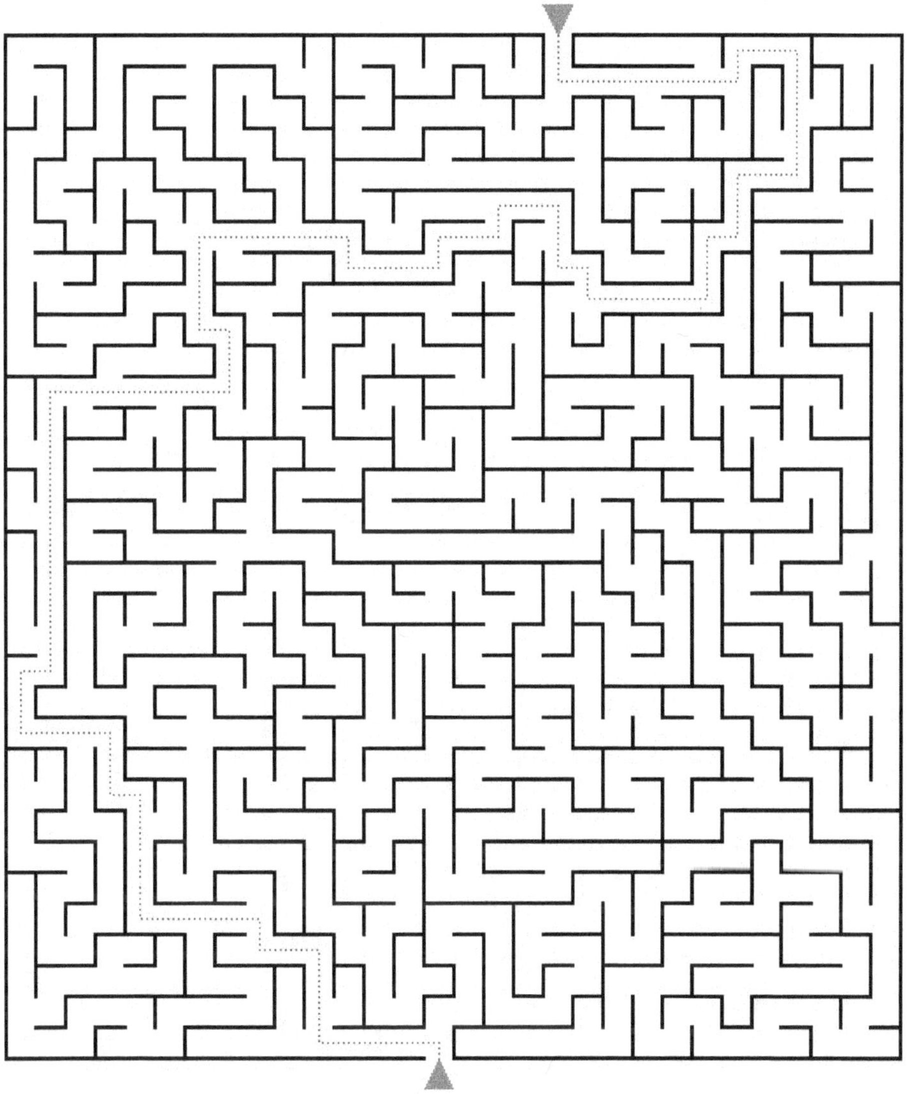

www.ingramcontent.com/pod-product-compliance
Lightning Source LLC
Chambersburg PA
CBHW081446220526
45466CB00008B/2520